Contents

Letters from the
Carpenter's Wife

Glacier Bay Lodge
Bartlett Cove
Gustavus, Alaska
99826

① Sunday Feb 6 - 1972

After 2 weeks of beautiful weather
we now have an Alaskan blizzard
again. good thing it is sunday,
so lets hope it will blow over, instead of lasting for nearly a week like
it did the last time - I suppose
if a person lived here + had to work
for a living the weather would really

Letters from the
Carpenter's Wife

Glacier Bay Lodge, Alaska
Winter of 1971-72

Leah Allender

Editors
Mimi Allender
Ken Allender

Illustrations & Design
Mark Allender

Publisher
Senton Design

www.sentondesign.com/books/lftcw
sentondesign@gmail.com

In Memoriam

Leah Allender
1916 – 2000

Jack Allender
1916 – 1999

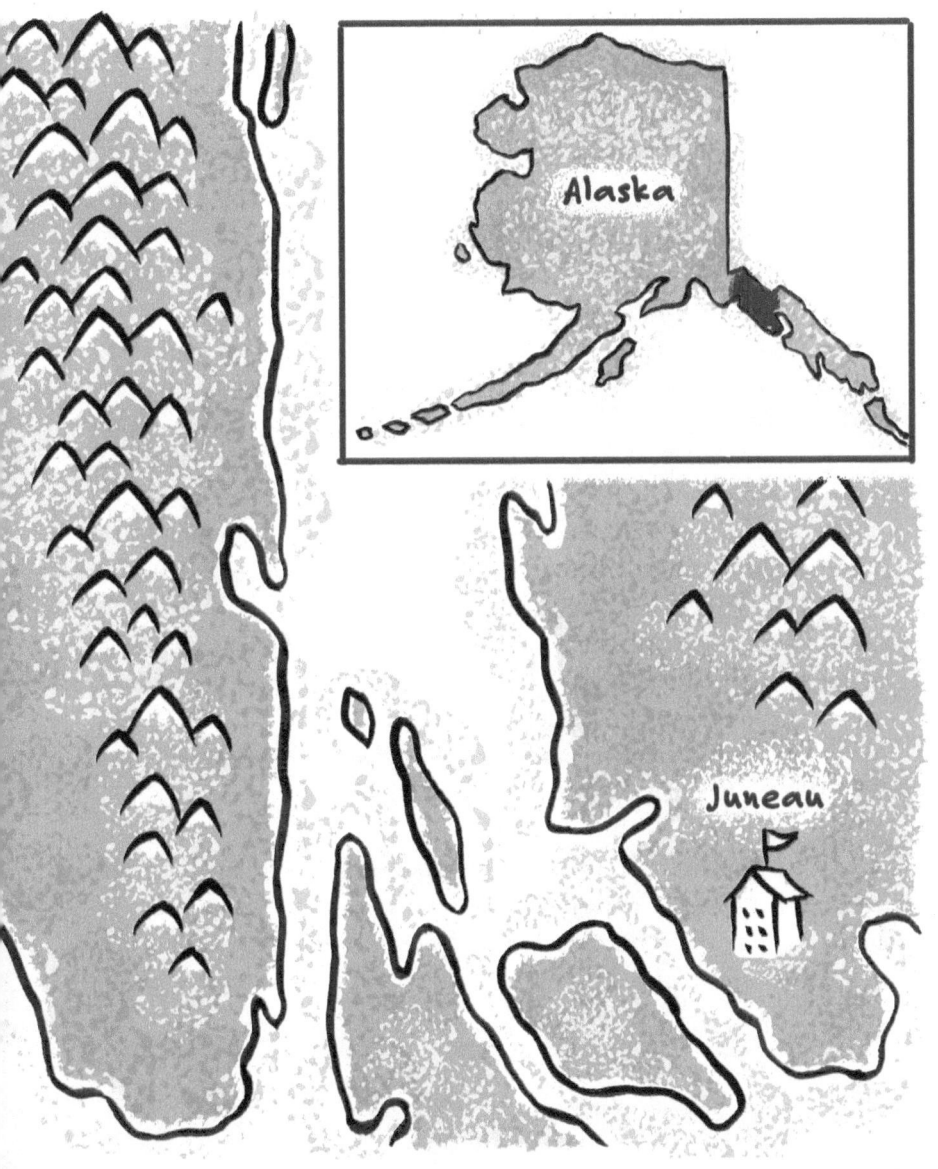

Foreword

"What about this?" my wife, Mimi, asked. She held up a small flat department store gift box, masking tape peeling on several sides, 'Alaska letters' written in pencil on its top. With an eye toward lightening the load, we were sorting through the family memorabilia that collects in the dark corners of closets.

And I knew immediately what that small box held: my mother's correspondence from Glacier Bay Lodge in Bartlett Cove, Alaska, during the winter of 1971-72. My dad, Jack Allender, had been hired as the carpenter foreman for a lodge expansion project.

My mother, Leah Allender, would assist in the kitchen, but mostly she expected to enjoy a winter vacation in a winter wonderland. The letters, 128 handwritten pages, hadn't been read for over 50 years. Our discovery occurred just prior to taking our fourth Alaskan trip where we again cruised Glacier Bay on a beautiful sunny day. The vacation inspired us to investigate the letters further.

We found them engaging and cleverly written, an adventure recounted by Leah, "the carpenter's wife," and we realized that others might also enjoy her tale as well.

Jack had recently "retired" at the age of 55 from his long term employment in the Centralia, WA, area. He and Leah, also 55, had rented their home for the duration of the project so were homeless other than their room at Glacier Bay and as guests of Leah's sisters back home.

Although many details and background information are now lost to time, we know that Jack was offered the foreman carpenter position by a Kent, WA, contractor to build 37 chalets (cabin rooms) at the Glacier Bay Lodge, nine miles west of Gustavus on the entrance to the bay. He was recruited by the Kearns family, some of whom lived in Centralia. The Park Service contracted the construction of the lodge and chalets, and Frank Kearns (and a few other silent partners) had obtained a 25 year concession for the lodging, and were to purchase the lodge and cabins from the Park Service through installment payments.

The catch? Work needed to proceed in the winter so as not to interrupt lodge operation of hosting guests during the tourist season.

Fortunately, Leah documented the adventure via regular letters and diary entries to her children. That correspondence rotated through the three siblings and ended up in a small flat box in the corner of our closet.

With the exception of a couple notes from Jack, where noted, Leah wrote the bulk of this material. Other than some personal material that was omitted, we left the text as written with minor adjustments for clarity. And, since she had not much formal education, it's her English, not the King's English!

We used the Allender and Kearns names and changed a few others. While Leah was smitten with her Alaskan experience and was gracious in daily life, she was more candid in these family letters. That added to their character but required that we file off some sharp edges, and, as a result, a few colorful adjectives and comments were omitted.

- Ken Allender

Where's That Barge?

October 18, 1971:

Leah: Guess what! Yes, we are still on vacation. The barge has been in Juneau for a week, and we expect it every day, but it hasn't shown up yet. They flew to Juneau yesterday to see what was holding them up. They said nothing but the tide. They aren't here today. So I am afraid somewhere along the line someone is too lenient or does not know what he is doing. Then again, this is how most of the large companies run. Anyway, we are way behind schedule.

It is quite expensive to fly to Juneau. They charge so much per flight. Then it is divided between the passengers, so it sums between $10 to $15 one way. If you are the one and only passenger, it will cost you $60. But if the sky is clear, it is well worth it, as I do not know where you could see anything as beautiful. You fly right through the inlet and into Bartlett Cove.

I was all prepared to spend a very quiet and lonesome winter. But this place is as bad as Grand Central Station, and we never know how many we will have for dinner. The planes are in and out constantly with the big shots looking things over and making sure everything is okay. These guys employed by the national park are real go-getters.

Sorry, I am on duty again!

Jack: The barge left Juneau at 3:00 pm today and will arrive about 3:00 am. Has to be unloaded in 12 hours so will start early. Worked today on electrifications etc.

We went out the other afternoon and caught seven king salmon from 22 to almost 40 pounds apiece. Jim Kearns and I had the two biggest ones on at the same time. Some fun! Also got several halibut. I got one over 40 pounds. Five of us went to Bird Bay one day, walked a half mile to a small lake where they had a 14-foot boat, and caught about 20 silver salmon on light tackle. I also caught two big trout, one over five pounds.

We went for a hike yesterday to Bartlett Lake. No fish, but it was a beautiful trip. Mother went with us, walked about six miles. We will be working now, so won't get to fish much. Will go deer hunting when it snows.

Plane is going to Juneau, so I will get letters off a day early. The barge is six hours late, and they are trying to locate it. Hope it didn't sink!

October 21st:

Leah: Sally Kearns' Uncle Cy was here from California, a kind old gentleman. He swept the lodge for me. Did he ever love our swiss steak!

We really do like it here. The tourists are all gone, so there are just the 20 of us. But there is always something to do and time has flown. We are a very mixed group. Dad and I are the oldest. Then six boys, ages 18 to 24. Three girls, seven to 11, and three married couples.

October 22nd:

I did a little washing. The water here has some kind of minerals in it, and the clothes are all turning yellow. The dryer sure works nice and fast. Each one of us has to do their own washing, so the weekend is lined up with people washing. Someone is always up to some mischief.

October 23rd:

Hooray! I only worked five hours today. Andy, the 18-year-old cook, has been very depressed since Wednesday. He got 17 letters but none from home.

October 24th:

What a day! All is well. I only worked three hours today. Hope Andy feels better. Time for work. Today was Andy's day. Went over and no Andy, so I started to wash pots and pans. I heard some noise behind but did not bother to look.

Before I knew it, I was swept off my feet, smothered in kisses, and Andy saying, "I just talked to my mom and dad!" His voice was jubilant. "Yes, they called me, and I am the happiest boy alive!"

"You are homesick and lonesome for your parents," I said.

Then he admitted he was, and that he missed his two sisters and two brothers very much. They live in Mesa, Arizona.

He explained he went out on his own at the age of 15, came here to Bartlett Cove, and has worked here during the summer until he graduated from high school last summer. He was offered the cook job here for the winter and took the offer.

They have a very large trampoline here at the lodge, and in July Andy was acting up on it, hit the side rail, and broke his neck in three places. He was in the Seattle Hospital (Virginia Mason) until September. Then he took this cook job.

"Believe me, I have learned a lot about myself, not knowing the outcome of the accident," he said.

They did not think he would walk before the end of one year, and he was up and out of the hospital by the end of three months.

Oh! The bears are at my window again. Mama Bear is so black and baby bear is very cute. They are just sitting there and looking at me through the window. They are crawling up the tree, now down. Baby Bear evidently did not do as his mama said, so she slapped him. Yes, on the behind!*

See #3 in 'A Little Extra' for more about black bears.

The walkways up to the lodge are all built up on cement pillars with side railings, so if a bear is around, there is no fear as they cannot get at you.

Time to cook dinner. We have five guests tonight, so we'll have some cooking to do.

Hooray! First snow of the year and the kids are enjoying it.

Oops, just stepped out the door and got hit in the head by a hard snowball! That Andy is back to his old self again! I am glad his parents called. I could certainly write a book on our stay here, but I wasn't born to be an author, so please accept me as I am. But if I were an author, Andy would be my main topic, as he is the most inspirational person here. He runs this lodge which is too much responsibility for so young a lad.

October 25th:

Had a good snow blizzard last night and this morning. It cleared up this pm and talk about beautiful! I have never seen the sun's reflection change the mountains as it does here. It is 32° at 6:00 pm. I saw the whale again today.

We had barbecued moose ribs tonight. It is just as good as beef.

We are going to watch Bill Mason's pictures tonight.

October 26th:

Nice and crisp today, about 18 above zero. The snow and mountains are still very graceful. No one here at the lodge has ever spent a winter here at Bartlett Cove, so we are preparing cars for the winter which caught us all unprepared. It has been many years since they have had snow (about one foot) plus this cold this early.

Just on awakening, I thought why didn't I snap pictures of the bears looking in my window?

Yes, as I said, Andy is feeling better. He grabbed a two-foot-long carving knife and came at me with it, saying, "I am a navel stabber," with a grin on his face from ear to ear.

I said, "You stab me, and that will be the end of you."

Then he went to Myke and said, "I am a navel stabber today."

And just then in walks the pregnant Mrs. Kearns, and he pointed the knife at her and said, "I am a navel stab-." He did not get the word out and said, blushing, "No, I get two navels, wouldn't I?"

She couldn't help but laugh and said, "Oh, Andy, I give up on you!"

October 27th:

Today is letter day. The one day of the week that everyone looks forward to. It's a cold day, and we had to put Visqueen (plastic sheets) on the dining room windows so we wouldn't freeze. Our dining area is all windows.

Work is progressing, and the men's appetites are good. The cooks are busy and tired tonight. So the 27th of October was a busy and fast day. The mountains change from day to day and are most beautiful in winter.

October 28th:

For some reason or other I did not sleep last night. I think it is because the vertebrae between my shoulders are out from all the heavy sweeping and lifting of those big, heavy pots and pans. Went to work this morning and passed out on the job.

I have slept nearly all day and feel much better now. I could have slept better if someone wouldn't be here every few minutes to check on me! I am sure it isn't serious, so have no worries.

We only have about six hours of daylight here, so the men aren't worked to death. But that is long enough in this miserable weather. They say later on it will get colder and nicer, not so much of this sleet. None of the men are complaining and seem very compatible.

Yes, our mail arrived this morning, and I received your package, Betty, and it was okay. It looks very graceful on my desk. Many thanks.

The wind is blowing terrible today, and I am watching the men work from my cabin window. You never know, maybe there will be a time when our lights will go out, and your candle will come in handy. At least I will be prepared.

October 29th:

The lodge has lots of reading material, so I am doing my share of reading although Dad reads two to my one. It's good relaxation for my breaks. In the evenings the men play Pinochle or chess or pool. You name it and it is here.

The men came in at lunch time very jubilant about the work that was accomplished. The cement truck did not break down even if it is only working on three cylinders. They have had lots of trouble with it. One day they only poured two yards.

Andy baked six cakes this morning for the Gustavus Halloween party and cake walk Halloween Eve. I do not believe I will go, as I do not feel too sharp yet from my fainting spell. But I am back to work, as Andy can not handle the kitchen by himself.

Talk about a happy go lucky kid! He made up a song about my name. "Leah Pe-deah, how about coming to see-ya!" He is the life of the party, and, I might add, 6'2" tall, dark, and very handsome, and a personality that everyone loves.

Jack: Hope a plane goes to town in a day or two. They haven't flown much this week, as we had a blizzard Sunday night and Monday morning. We didn't go to work until Monday noon. Eight inches of snow, but we are rid of about half of it now. It rained today. We haven't done much for entertainment lately, as we have had to work. I want to go deer hunting soon. We will go to an island that is supposed to be real good.

October 30th:

Leah: I warned Dad not to mention my birthday to anyone, but these men are worse than women. They had cake, trimmings and all, plus a pair of house slippers from everyone. Andy kept singing "Happy Birthday" into my ear all day long. I was quite embarrassed.

Our snow is gradually leaving us, and they finally got the boat out of the bay today to store for winter. Sunday is a lazy and restful day — for the men!

October 31st:

Andy added the finishing touches to my birthday dinner. What a dinner! Turkey, dressing, mashed potatoes, gravy, cranberries, fruit salad, pickles, rolls just out of the oven. Plus pumpkin pie with whipped cream. What hearty appetites!

It rained this morning but is clear and cold tonight. If it freezes, it will be quite a hindrance to the cement work, as they are now about 3/4 done with the pillars.

Wish we could share some of our lovely smoked salmon with you. The fishermen had to stop fishing, as all the deep freezes are full plus more smoked fish than we will ever be able to eat. Ray had quite a time keeping the bears away from the smoke house.

Those marvelous Penney's boots lasted just one month, so Dad had our pilot who is staying here at the lodge get him a pair from Juneau. They cost $27, but they are a real pair of boots.

Frank Kearns came back after three days in Seattle. He said the weather was cold there, and that second barge had not left Seattle yet. I guess they do not travel the dangerous channel unless they are filled. I have heard so many excuses I just give up.

King Crab, Anyone?

November 1st:

Andy made fudge and fudge plus caramels for Halloween. How luscious, my weakness!

Today is a beautiful day and work is progressing, so the men are in good moods. Frank Kearns flew to Juneau to get the men some new rain clothes plus gloves, as they do not last too long with rugged wear.

I haven't seen my mama bear plus her baby for a week now. I guess the snow rushed them into hibernation. To watch it snow here is quite different than at home, as the snow is always blowing sideways. That is, going north or west with the wind.

November 2nd:

Epidemic hits Glacier Bay Lodge! The flu went around Gustavus and through the schools. The kids brought it home from school. Today Dad, Jim Kearns, Ray Smith, Chuck Kearns, Bill Mason, Johnda Mason, John Kearns, and Jenny and Julie Kearns all suddenly came down with it. Several others aren't feeling too well. Food tonight? Simple.....soup.

Awoke this morning, we have snow again, and, oh, how that wind did howl! For the first time I was cold. I believe it was in my mind rather than actually being cold, as the wind just whistled.

They have some Alaskan tours in their magazines here, so Dad has been busy reading. We will very likely see most of Alaska before coming home unless we get very homesick. I doubt very much if we will come home except for Christmas, as we both still just love it here. No one hustles and bustles. Dad says it's the easiest job he has ever had in his life, and he is thoroughly enjoying it. All the Kearnses are very easy going, take life as it comes, and do not get too excited.

One of the young workers, Karl, is having a problem. He is asking for help from Andy. I do hope Andy can help him, as he definitely needs help. He is a hippie-looking person now, but I am sure if he cleaned up and had a decent haircut and shave, I believe he would be a very attractive man. I am going along and doing all I can for him, but there really isn't anything anyone can do. He himself will have to make the adjustment. He has tried to bribe Andy and pay him outrageous prices for whiskey. But Andy is as honest as they come, therefore, no deal. Last night the two had a conference. This conference and the problems are respected and kept private.

In case I haven't mentioned it before, we have a large bar here, as large as you can find anywhere. It is a great money-making deal, especially during the summer for those sportsmen. Of course, now it is closed and locked up, and Andy and I are the only ones allowed to go in. I guess their liquor laws are quite rigid here. They are looking for a bartender for next summer and are hinting around for someone to take it.

November 3rd:

Mail day! If it is too bad of a day, the mail will come by boat, the Forrester. It will bring freight plus our third class mail to Gustavus from Juneau. The pilots here respect the weather, the rough water they have to land on, and, most important of all, their lives. It is very interesting listening to the stories of the bush pilots*, and Gilley, our pilot, can tell them! Their planes have to be in perfect condition, and with this bad weather here, he works on his plane all the time. He has to keep it free of ice at all times. His throttle froze the other morning!

The epidemic flu is still continuing at Glacier Bay Lodge. No work, as the wind is blowing too much and it is just plain cold.

I have often wondered how an epidemic or plague could wipe out small settlements. I have found out. We had two snowy, cold, blistery and windy days, and four took sick during the night with a stomach virus. By the next day six more came down, including your dad. Andy, he says he never gets sick. Poor Andy, sick bay today. Yes, and with the flu. So Leah and Frank are head cook and bottle washer.

Now they're all down but us three women, the boss, and one other kid. Believe me, it makes you think. But we all pull together as one and take turns in doing the work. They are a marvelous bunch of people, and we have learned a lot from them.

* See #4 in 'A Little Extra' for more about bush pilots.

November 4th:

Today we will have to celebrate Herb's birthday since most were too sick yesterday. His favorite, custard pie.

The weather has cleared again and it is beautiful. When it is clear, there is no more beautiful sight than Bartlett Cove. It's the clouds and the low sun effects.

Dad and Jim Kearns are ahead of the cement crew. So guess what? Yes, we get to fly over the Fairweather Mountains and glaciers today. Our bush pilot just okayed it. Yippee! I am going, too, and it will be a double shift day, but that's okay.

We returned from our mountain flight. Wow! What a trip! A couple of times my stomach came up, and I got dizzy from the flight, as we were trying to watch a large hunk of glacier break off and fall into the ocean. That will be some sight when it does. We took around 150 pictures between the three of us.

I remember one time I watched an Alaskan bear expedition on TV, never dreaming I would be up in an airplane gliding around to see what is below. We saw icebergs with seals on top relaxing. We flew close to the goat rocks, so I had a thrill there! I am sure Dad would have loved to land and done some hunting.

Flying between these treacherous mountains made you think, and we asked the pilot if those seaplanes could land on the snow. He said no. You either land on water or else you have had it, as you could never survive the cold.

These bush pilots are highly trained and take no chances. They have their earphones on, and we are in contact with their station at all times. Most of the planes hold six people, five passengers and the pilot. It costs $100 an hour to charter this plane. They fly around 160 miles per hour. Therefore, you can see a lot of scenery in a short time.

November 5th:

It was a very nice day, and the men all worked. We are still waiting for that second barge to arrive. Andy is back on his feet again, I hope the flu epidemic is over, and that the women have escaped it.

I do not know why, but Dad's and my clothes are both shrinking away. Pretty soon we will not be able to wear them at all.

I guess Karl is having a party tonight. Yes, we are next door to each other. I hope the furniture will last, and they will quiet down before midnight. You can hear everything in these cabins, as they are not well insulated between cabins.

November 6th:

Surprise! Again this morning we woke up to four inches of snow and still snowing. It's a detriment to the working men and cement works, but they will have it licked within a few days. The snow here is whiter and much prettier than on the highways, as it falls and stays and no cars or men to dirty it.

The flu bug hit Myke today, and Andy called his mother to wish her a happy birthday, the 40th, but he has been depressed since.

Saturday night, the big night for Pinochle and chess. Karl had a party next door with some of the other younger guys. I thought they were tearing down the place.

November 7th:

I slept in this morning. When I came to the lodge, Andy for some reason or other was still blue, so I told him to go for a long walk and think things out. I would do all the kitchen work today. Poor kid is so homesick and is looking forward to Christmas when he can go home.

The Kearns kids' teacher came to see the lodge today. He is a young gentleman, just married, and with one child. He has short hair and a goatee. He evidently is very good from what I hear. It's just a one-room schoolhouse with all the grades.

The men went bird hunting today. Leslie Kearns just got up here, and he is letting his hair and beard grow. His hair is sort of reddish, but his beard is real red. But Dad makes the best hippie of all.

November 8th:

Another day of leisure. The pillar foundations are in, and we are still waiting for that second barge. I guess this is what is wrong with this whole world. Nothing is run on schedule, you just do things as the spirit moves you, and if it is when or what you care to do.

Mrs. Kearns told Andy he was over budget for this month. He is allowed $1,000 per month for the 20 of us. The things that go in the garbage bucket make me shudder. I could live like a queen on it. So many people do not realize you can cook good meals and still cook economically. It's not what you cook, but how, and the amount you cook and the waste.

The coyotes were busy singing last night, and it sends a shiver right up your spine. Then you flip the cover over your head, and you have that comfortable feeling that you are safe.

I do not know if I ever described our cabins. They are really deluxe. A large bedroom and front room combined. We have two double beds with a table between them and a suitcase holder at the end of the beds. Then we have a nice desk with a mirror, an end table with a large lamp, and the base of the lamp is covered with brown leather. One easy chair, one upright chair, a waste paper basket. There's a ladder that goes to the loft with a twin bed and where we store our suitcases. We have a nice bathroom with a shower. The entrance hall consists of a closet, a chest of drawers, and shelves. We have lots of room. It's 16 by 20 feet, and our furniture is all solid white oak.

I have it fixed real cute. One wall I covered with all the nice cards we have received while here. Above the beds I have lovely pictures of Alaska. One wall is all windows. The cabin colors are brown and orange with cedar paneling and 4"x14" open beams. So we are very comfortable.

Time does fly, and we have been here nearly a month already. Lately, I have not even found the time to write and have just sent my daily notes. I hope you will all save them, as this place is very interesting. So much happens every day that I just sort of keep a diary. After nine months up here, it would make a very nice book or reading material.

November 9th:

It is a very clear and beautiful day. The men are still on vacation. No barge. They went fishing today and saw lots of fish, but they could not get them to bite. Dad and Jim Kearns brought in a load of firewood and looked for deer tracks but only found coyote and bear tracks. Later, they decided to go hunting, but Bill Mason could not get his boat to run. So they could not get across the bay. What a disappointment for them.

I showed Andy how to make an egg carton Christmas tree.*

November 10th:

It is another beautiful day, and the men are still on vacation as no sign of the barge yet. They caught a bunch of fish today, just don't know what to do with them. They caught dollies and trout up to six pounds. I guess the other men have more fun watching Dad catch them, as he gets so excited than it is for them to catch them.

We are feeding a marten to keep him around. They are interesting to watch. I guess our bears hibernated.

Sally Kearns went to Juneau to the doctor today. Andy went to an art class at Gustavus. So I took it easy, too. I would love to go to Juneau and spend a couple of days while the men are not working, but it costs $20 one way.

We are being serenaded today. Next door Karl is trying his best to learn to play the guitar and sing. And through these paper thin walls! Boy, oh, boy! It's hard on the nerves.

It reminds me of when I used to sing at home, and you boys would say, "Oh, Mother."

* See #2 in 'A Little Extra' for Leah's tuna can Christmas tree.

It wouldn't do to say that to Karl. This goes on for hours and night after night after night, the same thing. If he could just halfway carry a tune.

November 11th:

Today is the long-awaited day. The second barge arrived at about 4:00 pm. I am afraid the men's vacations are over. In order to tell you how large the barge is, I will tell you its cargo. It has all the material for 37 chalets. This includes the framework (rough structure) plus all the way through to the shakes and finish material. Plus plumbing and also all the furniture..

Some of the men are playing bridge tonight. I guess Dad and I will have to learn how. It certainly is a good pastime, as when the men leave the dinner table, they immediately start a game of some kind.

The enlargement of the bar was discussed today, and Frank Kearns asked Ray to be the bartender. He accepted with great pleasure. Ray is a very quiet person, and he comes from a wealthy family. His dad is a doctor in Mesa, Arizona. Ray is a tall, blond, 6'3" gentleman. A lot of these Mormon men are tall and very good looking, personality the best.

It seems so comical to me when any of them go anywhere, which isn't far, since there are only ten miles of road, they always ask me to go along.

The man caught fish galore today. They had to turn about ten salmon loose. We are going to smoke these and bring some home for Christmas. Our beautiful weather has ended, and it is raining tonight, but it is very warm.

November 12th:

What a day! Unloading of the barge! The cooks have to be on schedule again making food for the meals and breaks. I just cannot resist all this marvelous food. We have absolutely everything for the men, even ice cream. We do not lack one thing. Eggs cost $1 per dozen, steak close to $2 per pound. The food really isn't much higher in Juneau. It's the nine cents per pound that we have to pay to have it flown here. All our vegetables etc. we buy by the case, frozen. We bake all our own bread, rolls, hamburger buns etc. Andy is the best pie and donut baker there ever was.

It is overcast today but very warm. I took two pictures of the barge, one from the front and one from the rear. A barge in Bartlett Cove is quite something for the locals. Two of the big shots from the construction company are coming in at 2:00 pm today. It is a 24-hour job to get the barge unloaded, so they are working in shifts. It will be a great relief for all when it is unloaded.

November 13th:

What a beautiful, glorious day! The men worked all day and all night until 7:30 am. Then you should have seen the sunrise on this nice clear day. The barge left at high tide about 9:00 am. Now no more leisure for the men, as we are way behind. Everyone is so cooperative and not one lazy person in the crowd. So everything is going beautiful.

The bay is calm as could be and just filled with seals today. But you cannot get close enough to get a picture. I haven't seen the bear or marten lately. The bald eagles have been keeping the fisherman company, as the fishermen are in the eagles' food hole, and they do not like it. One made a dive at Jim Kearns.

November 14th:

Andy's day off and I have to prepare the three meals by myself. It's a workout.

The men got the barge unloaded and then took off for fishing. They took out the architect and the surveyor. They came home with 37 dollies from two to five lbs, so we have had fish for two days. They sure are good.

Our martens* are back and running around the porch railing. I have been feeding them to keep them near. They are so pretty with long fur. The seals are too smart. You cannot get close to them to get a picture.

November 15th:

It's a nice warm day, and the men made some progress on the chalets. Our architect tried to leave today, but evidently the water was too turbulent in Juneau to land, although the water was very calm here. So you never know. Sometimes it takes three to four days before anyone can come in or leave in the winter time. The bush pilots are very careful, because if they crack up in those little planes, that's it!

Andy and I baked bread today, and fresh cinnamon rolls, sugar cookies, apple pie. I can sure feel it tonight.

* See #5 in 'A Little Extra' for more about the marten.

Lorraine Kearns called tonight. I guess she is lonesome for Jim, so she may come up for Thanksgiving. If so, I may go back home with her to see if Dr. Park can help make me feel better. I have not felt good at all these last two weeks. I just hate to leave, but I have to find out what is wrong. Then I can come back with Dad on the 2nd of January.

November 16th:

Fairly warm, but cloudy. The men got quite a bit of work done. The department surveyor is still here. He is a big blonde Swede with a very hearty appetite. He is from Seattle. He does not like the short, rainy days. The weather hasn't cooperated since he is here. I hope it will clear, so he can see those beautiful mountains and the miracles of the sun.

Dad and I are both learning bridge. It seems quite complicated. We quit at 11:00 pm, had a milkshake, and went to bed.

November 17th:

It really started to rain this pm, and the surveyor only worked about four hours, as the weather wasn't cooperating. But the carpenters all worked, and they were hungry. They ate our two baked hams in raisin sauce plus the banana cream pie just like they were savages.

Andy goes to Juneau tomorrow to see the doctor about his broken neck. He will stay with a friend there and have a blind date for Friday night. Is he ever excited!

Today was mail day, and it came just before lunch. We sorted it and put it on the dinner table. Instead of eating first, they opened their mail and let the food get cold. It was real comical to hear one or the other say:

"Oh, I heard from my girlfriend."

"What do you know! I heard from my little brother."

"Gee, my other girlfriend loves me, too. Now what am I going to do?"

"Just look at my letter my mother wrote and only enclosed one sheet. I am left in the air just when her letter got interesting. Maybe she will enclose it in her next letter."

On and on, the whole dinner time.

Tonight Dad and Jim are out with flashlights trying to find alder wood to smoke the fish, and it is just pouring down rain. I will take smoked fish home with me. Then I will send you some. It is so unhandy to send packages from here. I have some smoked fish packaged but haven't been able to send it. Mildew will not hurt it, as it is preserved like cheese.

November 18th:

I have the kitchen all to myself since Andy is at Juneau. Talk about a workhouse.

Jim Kearns called his wife, and she is coming up for Thanksgiving. So we just sat in our cabins gossiping tonight. The weather was fair and the men were hungry.

We had swiss steak, 20 large ones. Leslie Kearns felt sorry for me and did wipe the utensils. We have a dishwasher for the dishes, and Myke does that, but I have to wash all the heavy cooking utensils. Some are so heavy I can hardly lift them.

Jack: We went for a ride to Gustavus and stopped at the fishing hole on the Salmon River but only got one trout about six pounds. Too cold to fish.

November 19th:

Leah: It was an exceptionally warm day. Sally took Frank to the airport at Gustavus and hadn't returned, so Myke and myself got quite worried, thinking she had a flat tire on her VW. Myke went looking for her and found her visiting with the wives of the park maintenance personnel.

The surveyor, Dan, is quite a guy. He washed all the pots and pans for me tonight and also packed food down to the storage room. He thought I was doing too much. I only put in 12 hours today. Will be glad when Andy gets back!

November 20th:

Just another day of work, was nice and warm this morning, but now this afternoon it is snowing. The carpenters had to get busy and cover their lumber with Visqueen.

Homemade bread is really something around here, so I baked eight loaves this morning. But by tomorrow it will all be gone.

Herb, the boss for the construction company who has the contract for these chalets, is quite a guy. He can live on fresh bread and coffee. No wonder he has ulcers. He is very easy to get along with, is the first one to be on the chow line, and the last one to get up in the morning. In fact, Dad darn near has to break his door down to get him awake. Yet he says he never sleeps.

I asked him who his bed partner was that did all that snoring. He had to laugh and stated, "Well, when I do fall asleep, I really sleep."

With Karl on one side, his guitar and off-key singing, plus Herb on the other side with his snoring, I'd say we were entertained at all times.

Joy, joy, joy! Time to put the stuffed pork chops in the oven. So we'll slide over to the lodge, as those wood walks are all ice. The kids have lots of fun sliding on them.

November 20th:

Saturday night, so we had a party. Jim popped the popcorn, and Karl cut out some building blocks. The old and the young sat on the floor building block houses, forts, and the Eiffel Tower. When the tower was about completed, Dan, the engineer, sneaked upstairs and got a pool ball, and all of a sudden — disaster to the tower!

The smallest Kearns girl got mad at her sister, and she said, "I am so mad at you, I am going to show you my teeth." She has buck teeth.

The sister said, "Oh, no, anything but that!"

Then later on she got mad again, and she said, "I am not going to speak to you for five whole minutes." Every minute she kept asking if the five minutes were up, so she could speak to her again. The kids are a joy to have around, as they are so well mannered in every way.

November 21st:

The men's day of leisure. Why couldn't a woman be born with one day of leisure or else why couldn't I have been born a boy, man or gentleman. Oh, well, guess I will have to be satisfied just to be born.

Dan, our engineer, was a gentleman today and shelled ten pounds of shrimp for me which helped me a great deal. So we will have shrimp creole tomorrow. Glacier Bay has beautiful king crab about two feet across and all this lovely shrimp we will have tomorrow.

Poor Dad had a rough day. He slept until 9:30 and ate a hearty breakfast. Then the rest of the day he spent fishing, reading, more sleeping, and more eating. Then he looks in the kitchen at 7:00 pm, sees me surrounded in pots and pans, and asks if there is anything he could do. Needless to say, he just got a cold stare, as I was about ready to drop.

November 22nd:

Today Andy came back from Juneau, and reports about his broken neck aren't too good. He has to go back for more x-rays.

If my writing is offbeat, that is because Karl is off two beats, one on guitar plus voice. I never knew anyone could sing so off key.

It was a real nice warm day, and the men have quite a bit accomplished. Herb and Dan ate the shrimp creole as if it was their last meal. How they love to eat! Dad isn't even in it.

Since Andy is back, I will take off a few hours a day and do my washing and ironing, wash my hair, plus clean the cabin. Gee, isn't it nice to get off a few hours occasionally.

We have a red squirrel that is quite tame. He is the cutest guy and so proud.

I am between the devil and the deep blue sea. The Kearns want me to take the head cook job just in case Andy cannot take it after his next doctor's appointment. Lorraine Kearns is coming up from Centralia to spend Thanksgiving with us.

Today is rather windy, and we are preparing a big Thanksgiving dinner with absolutely all the trimmings. So work, work, here I come!

November 24th:

What a beautiful morning! The northern stars were dancing beautifully! I am so happy for the nice day, as Lorraine Kearns is coming in from Centralia, and I want her to enjoy the floatplane trip.

Lorraine arrived, and she was all bundled up for Alaska weather. Chuck, Jim Kearns' brother and roommate, silently moved out and moved into Herb's room, our boss, the contractor and snorer. What men won't do. They were teasing Jim Kearns who hadn't seen Lorraine since we left, so they made sure they had privacy.

Also, some of the surveyors, carpenters and National Park Board problems were discussed. It is so nice to have people sit down, give their different opinions, and then decide on the majority without even anyone raising their voice.

I was tired and retired early.

November 25th:

Thanksgiving Day. Awoke to find fresh snow and the wind blowing. Some of the men are working. It is quite a chore working with and against the weather. In other words, a challenge. Dad and Karl have about 1/3 of all the framing done, so from now on they will make headway before everything freezes and stays frozen all winter.

We are having a 35 lb turkey today with all the trimmings plus mincemeat, pumpkin, pecan pie, and cranberry bread. Food, food, and so much going to waste. Pure butter is used for anything and everything. I got out of being the cleanup person tonight! Gee, that felt good!

Lorraine and I played Pinochle with Dad and Jim tonight. Guess what! We skunked them! Hurray!

I showed Andy how to make a starburst out of all those gallon cans they have here. He just about has one completed.

10:30 pm: Most everyone is tired and another work day tomorrow.

November 26th:

It is a cold, blustery morning. It snowed about 1/2 inch, but that wind is so cold, everyone put on their 100 percent wool underwear.

Lorraine is freezing to death, and so she put on Jim's woolies. So far it hasn't bothered me. I am wearing the same clothes I wear at home.

I hear an airplane, so excuse me, as I have to go see who is coming in.

I investigated, and it was a seaplane plus a boat with 12 Bahias. You have probably heard of them. It is one of the new religions. They are going to give a service and show a movie of what the Bahia faith is tonight.

First, I spelled the word wrong. It's Baha'i. There were 12 young people and an old blind Eskimo. Did they ever have a good program! These people consisted of every race and color and from all over. A young school teacher and his wife were in charge. There was no minister. These kids strived hard to do this, as it takes money to charter a big boat and a sea plane. This all comes out of their pocket. They are taking in all the back country destinations they do not know.

Wherever they see smoke, they will pull in to see if anyone wants to listen. Then their musician comes in on the sea plane. He was their main singer, plus a Negro boy about 19 who was very good, and also an Indian. Then they had a beautiful young girl about 18 from California. The blind Eskimo did a song and dance with his drum.

November 27th:

I am supposed to have time off today. It will be the third day that I have had time off since we arrived. I have refused the head cook job, as Andy does have to go home. His broken neck did not heal right. He went back to work too soon. We are all going to miss him a great deal. I'll miss his affection, our waltzes, and just plain talk.

They are getting a cook out from Juneau. When I return after Christmas, I will have more leisure time, I hope! At least the Kearnses are concerned for me and want me to take it easier.

If it gets light enough today, I will take a picture of Dad and his men working, as it is a real Alaskan sight. It is 9:00 am, and they are working by lights with a small campfire going to keep their hands from freezing plus the 2x4s (lumber) they are working with. It is really snowing beautifully, and the snow is coming down nearly straight. Also, we have about two to three foot icicles hanging down from the roofs. A beautiful sight.

1:30 pm: I went out to take pictures and didn't have boots high enough, so I took someone's sitting in the lodge. What a break for me! I got out okay, was going to step over a little farther to get the light in the picture, and the ice on the bottom of the snow over the ditch gave way. You never heard such a loud cry from a woman in your life! There the men stood laughing for all they were worth, wishing they would have had a camera to take my picture instead. I hope my pictures will turn out okay. It was dark, but it had stopped snowing.

Lorraine Kearns and I plan on flying out as soon as possible. Dan, the engineer, is flying out also and is going to take us under his wing. If everything goes okay, we will leave on Wednesday, December 1st. Dad and the rest of the men will leave here on the 19th or 20th. Reservations are all made, if the weather will just accommodate.

November 28th:

Andy's day off, and I had to do all the cooking today. Lorraine and I wanted to go fishing with the men, so I hurriedly baked my pumpkin bread, made my pie crusts, and stuck the roast in the oven.

Then away we went in about a foot of snow. We had trouble with the chains but finally got them fixed and went fishing. But no fish today!

So Jim, Lorraine, Leslie, Dad, and I went joy riding in the snow. Then Dan, the engineer, joined us, and we spent two lovely hours of just simple fun. Karl hitched a sled to his car and took all the kids sledding. They kept passing and honking at us, and we also passed two trucks belonging to the park department. So we darn near had a traffic jam!

Walking the river with the fishermen, Lorraine and I darn near froze our feet off. We had so many clothes on we could hardly stoop or step up into the truck. And with Dan around there is never a dull moment.

You should have seen the food they devoured at dinner! No one had eaten pumpkin bread* before. Needless to say, it all went, and everyone wants the recipe. And nearly everyone had two helpings of lemon pie. Some of the evening was spent on the floor in front of the fireplace playing with the building blocks.

Lorraine and I beat Dad and Jim now in three consecutive evenings in Pinochle. One hand last night we made 730, and tonight our best hand was 610. Each time they got a bid, they would go set. Poor guys!. I actually felt sorry for them. It's bedtime… good night!

See #1 in 'A Little Extra' for a pumpkin bread recipe.

November 29th:

It is a dreary but quite warm day. No flights in and out of Juneau today. I surely hope Wednesday will be a nice day so we can fly out.

Lorraine and I watched the crab fishermen pull up those big crab pots, wishing we had some of those crab. For Lorraine and Dan's sake we had deep fried halibut balls. Did they ever eat!

Lorraine said it was a good thing she was leaving, or else she would be as big as a barrel. I used to have three rolls across the you-know-what. I now have four and a half going on five rolls. I can't hardly stoop. I had to give up scrubbing on my hands and knees. Now I do it like a lazy person, with a mop!

I was going to show Dad how to wash his clothes while I am gone, as old helpless is more than helpless without me or my help. As I walked back into the lodge, there were two strange gentlemen talking to the Kearnses and Dad.

Then Dad said, "Leah, come here," and he showed me the biggest crabs* I have ever seen in my life.

The fisherman said, "I'll let you take one of them home, provided I can sit with you."

I said it was a deal. Then I got to talking to the fisherman. They wanted to use the telephone, and, in appreciation, they brought up four crabs. It was the same boat we watched earlier in the day, wishing we had some of the crab.

I asked them if we could give them dinner or a drink. They said, "No, thank you." They were very happy to give those crabs to us.

See #6 in 'A Little Extra' for more on king crab.

44

He said these crabs, two feet across, are too small, and we cannot sell them. I told them we had watched them today, wishing there was a way we could get some, and I told them they certainly answered our wish.

He said, "Would you like some more?"

I said, "You mean you have more small ones?"

He said, "Yes, I have six more in the boat. If you would like to have them, you are more than welcome."

All our faces lit up!

So until 11:30 at night seven of us cleaned the crab. They showed us how, and we all had a grand time. The men bought a fifth from the bar for $10 and gave this to the fisherman. Then the men were invited on board, and the fifth was opened. Needless to say, there wasn't much left for the fishermen!

In these backwoods there isn't such a thing as a stranger. Now these fishermen plan on stopping in whenever they come through. It looked like they could be father and son, but we did not ask. They told us of their experience when they ran the boat aground, and they thought they'd had it. With these tides you have to know what you are doing.

November 30th:

What a beautiful day! Lorraine is dumbfounded with all the beauty, as you can only see it on a clear day, and with the reflection of the sun, it changes every few minutes. I have never seen anything like this! It is very intriguing. It snows a little every other day or so, but today it is melting fast.

I hear the airplane with our groceries, so we'll have to go down to the pier and pick them up.

I am packing today to go home tomorrow, December 1st. We leave Juneau at 12:00 noon and arrive in Seattle at 2:00 pm. Lorraine has her car there, so we have a way of getting to Centralia.

Wow! What a sunset on those gorgeous snow-covered mountains! Snow is predicted for tonight, and the airport notified us that the planes may not fly tomorrow. Oh, well! Today is my last working day, so I will just relax and really enjoy the scenery.

The Kearnses asked me if I was coming back after Christmas. I said I would love to if they needed me since they are getting one of the best cooks in Juneau. He will handle the cooking all by himself. They said if I come back, they would pay me for my flight both ways and still pay me $3 an hour, as they did not want to lose me. They said I was so highly organized that I could get more work done in one day than two others they had ever hired. So that was quite a compliment! For an old, decrepit lady, I can still evidently do a little work.

Guess what we had for lunch today? Yes, crab louie, and were they ever good.

It turned cold tonight. Wonder what tomorrow will bring. It was a beautiful day, and the snow was melting this morning. It's unbelievable how the weather has changed. It got colder this evening. The sun was still out until sunset, but it kept on getting colder and colder, and now at 8:00 pm there is a terrible howling wind.

Everything is frozen solid, so we may not get out by plane. If not, Dan is going to get us on the first boat, the Nunatak. It will take us six hours to get to Juneau. Then maybe we can get out Thursday to Seattle. Wednesday evening he would take us to the Red Dog Bar in Juneau where they still have a sawdust floor.

Juneau Bound

December 1st:

A beautiful but disappointing morning. It snowed quite a bit last night. Therefore, we could not fly out to Juneau, nor are there any planes leaving Juneau today. So we decided to go on the Nunatak as it pulled in today.

Guess what! They have engine trouble, and it will take until noon tomorrow morning before they get it fixed. So now we will put in for an emergency flight, and they will come out whenever the visibility from here to Juneau clears up the first time. Gosh knows when that will be, but at any rate we have to be ready to leave within a few minutes, as the weather changes so rapidly.

It is beautiful here at Bartlett Cove, but our problem is between Gustavus and Juneau. There are some rough, jagged mountains and no visibility for these small planes. So I am not pushing the matter, as I want to get out of here alive.

I told Lorraine we should have taken an opportunity Tuesday when we had it. But she wanted to stay one more day. Well, we now have that opportunity and then some. She did not realize that the weather predicts all our doings.

It has been snowing about every other day for the last two weeks. So the work is way behind. I am just **the carpenter's wife**, but I can see it and it bothers me, knowing the company is going to lose money.

December 2nd:

At 5:00 am the alarm is ringing! I have to get up! Jim, Lorraine, Dad and I are traipsing down the hill in about 14 inches of snow, loaded with suitcases and smoked fish plus fresh crab. What a beautiful morning. We are not taking the Nunatak which they did not get fixed here at the lodge after all. Dan talked us into going with him in his boat so that we can get at least to Juneau. Then our chance of getting home is pretty good.

Since there was something electrical wrong with the boat, we did not have heat or lights. They tucked us into bunks until 9:00 am. Was it ever dark down there with no windows. Then we were told to go up and sit with the skipper. We had a front seat all the way to Juneau, but it was cold, 29 °. What a sunrise! I took quite a few pictures. But, oh, those dirty windows. This is a national park boat, and Dan works for the park department, so we had lots of extra honors on the boat. It took a little over six hours to get to Juneau by boat.

Then we had just a few minutes to get to the airport. They were calling our flight when we got there, but we made it! The plane was delayed 15 minutes because Dan had all his surveying equipment to take home. The pilot announced he was sorry there was a delay in takeoff because of excess baggage. The three of us just grinned and didn't say much.

The flight home was excellent. I sat with a woman from Petersburg, Alaska, and we got to talking. It was her husband that flew us into the lodge when we first arrived. They fly to the lodge to eat on Sundays. She also knew the crab fisherman, as they are from Petersburg, too. So it's a small world after all.

We arrived at the busy Seattle airport by 3:30, stopped to see Lorraine's sister, and I got to Mollie's (Leah's sister) house at 6:00 pm. No one was home. But I went in, washed my hair, and made myself at home.

December 3rd:

I am sitting in Dr. Park's office, hoping to get in. I am the second one here so should have a chance.

Finally made it in and have to go to a specialist, but I can not get in until next Saturday. So there I sit for another week.

The Sheriff Visits

January 3rd, 1972:

My month's vacation at home went fast, and I got a lot accomplished. I quilted my last quilt, just too much work, and also helped Bob (Leah's brother) refinish his kitchen and bathroom cupboards with the electric sander. The birch refinished real nice. Then, naturally, it led to cleaning the curtains, windows, and floors!

We left Centralia for Seattle on Monday at 6:00 am. The plane was supposed to leave at 8:00 am. It was a cold day in Seattle, but Juneau had a terrific snow storm, so they changed it to 9:30. In the meantime they had us get on the plane and have our breakfast. But we could not leave Seattle until 10:30 that morning.

We finally arrived in Juneau at 1:15. It really made you think, as the visibility was zero until we got close to the ground. We had a perfect landing, so all was well. But our California crew that came in afterwards had a very rough landing, and they said they did a little extra thinking!

Our new cook was there to meet us in Juneau. But we knew we could not fly out of Juneau, so we stayed at the cook's living quarters that night. There were only ten of us that flew in, the cook made us a nice dinner, and we slept on the window sills which are padded with foam pads. I was the only woman, so they all tried to wait on me. It's a good thing I know them quite well, so I did not feel too uncomfortable.

January 4th:

We had to be at the airport by 9:00 this morning. Alaska Airlines has a small plane that holds 18 passengers, and it's equipped with radar. They will fly us into the airport at Gustavus. It was snowing so hard we never saw one thing on this flight. We had a very smooth landing, so these pilots evidently know what they are doing.

All of Gustavus was out to meet us. The lodge had two trucks there to haul the ten of us to the lodge with all our luggage. It took them two trips to take us all back. We were shocked at how much more snow we have, at least four feet of snow, and it is still snowing. It took one day for the men to shovel off the snow so they could work. It is not cold at the present, and they are enjoying working in the snow.

I do not know how much snow there is here, but it's plenty. The steps have heat in them and are always clear, but they are surrounded with snow.

Karl, our hippie, is no longer a hippie. He got a haircut, his beard shaved off, and, as I suspected, he is a very handsome man.

Hardly anyone recognized him, and everyone remarked how handsome he is. So he is quite flattered. He said he hopes to go back to school one day, as he was earning good money here. He wants to stand on his own two feet again.

We are all behind him and hope he makes a go of it. He had his 22nd birthday yesterday, so we had a birthday cake and all. He seemed pleased.

January 5th:

While I was gone, they had to get help up here, so now I do not work long hours, just four hours a day. They got a newly graduated teacher who could not find a job. She is a good friend of the Kearnses. I am very happy over this new deal. I just helped the new cook a little, and by what I have seen so far he does not compare to Andy at all. He is just a nervous little old man who loves his drinks, and he has it hid all over. After working with him for a while, maybe I will change my mind. Time will tell.

Herb brought back a lather (drywall finisher) from Bremerton (WA). He is a young bearded man with four children. Everyone likes him very much. He doesn't drink or smoke, and he likes to tease people with his beard like Dad does. His hair isn't too short, and it's trimmed neatly. He gets along with everyone which is very important.

January 6th:

It has been snowing every day. The men have to dig themselves out. We can't keep our sidewalks clean, and it goes over my boots. I do not know how these cabins stand up. They have over three feet of snow on the roofs plus a two foot overhang of snow and ice from the end of the roof. It seems so comical to see the icicles hang down from the end of that instead of from the end of the roof. I am curious to know what will happen if that should break off.

January 9th:

A day of rest. Dad shoveled the snow off the sidewalks this evening. We again have about four inches of snow. Took some pictures of the snow, and the rest of the time the four of us tried to put a puzzle together, plus reading and washing.

10:00 pm: Will have to wash and set my hair yet.

January 10th:

It must have snowed all night, and we have one foot of new snow this morning. We'll dash fast-like to the lodge! We have five-foot icicles hanging down in front of our window.

Oops! My dash to the lodge wasn't very successful. I hit the first step and missed the next four and landed flat on my stomach. Good thing the new snow was soft. So many of us have taken good falls.

It's a regular blizzard this morning, the temperature zero. The men are working inside today. Herb is fighting a cold. Karl is trying to dig the truck out of four feet of snow so he can pick up Frank who has been stranded in Juneau since last Wednesday. It has snowed every day for one week now, and all told we have over five feet of snow.

It is absolutely beautiful, and I hope it will get light enough today so I can take some pictures. Since I do not work all day, I have more time to enjoy life.

We finished the puzzle. It was one of the hardest puzzles any of us had put together. I have a chance to read some of the books we brought along today.

What a blizzard! Since this morning we have three feet of snow on our walkway. No one has boots that high, so you just take off your boots, shake out the snow, and put them back on.

Dad has some frozen fingers this morning. The snowmobile boots he got while he was in Ellensburg (WA) are doing the trick. At least his feet are warm. This is the first time I have been cold.

January 11th:

It finally cleared up, and it's still one of the most beautiful spots in Alaska, even if it is too cold. No one has a thermometer, so we go by the news and what little the park board knows. We meant to pick up a thermometer when we were at home but forgot. It would be more interesting knowing how cold or warm it really was.

We should be prepared with heaters etc. so they could work inside in this cold weather. Well, they have nothing, So they are sitting around shooting the bull, playing cards, doing puzzles, movies etc. I told Dad to relax, as it wasn't our fault. So gosh knows when we will get done. John, our new lather, is beginning to crawl the walls. He has a wife and four children he would love to be with instead of sitting and eating all the time. He is a big brute and a worker.

January 12th:

Last night I believe was the coldest of all. We had to leave the water run all night again, as we have been having quite a bit of problems with the pipes freezing and breaking. The men are sitting around the fireplace. Our cabin is as warm as toast so I spend all my leisure time in it. I have so many letters to catch up on. Jim Kearns fell and twisted his knee, so I see him cleaning the sidewalk better, as they are terrible dangerous.

The martens are getting thick around here because we leave food out for them, but I have not been able to get a picture of one yet.

January 13th:

Still too cold to work. It's well below zero. Gustavus was 16 below last night, and that's only nine miles from here. Juneau was 20 below.

Our lodge roof started leaking today. The men had to climb up there and shovel the snow away from the vents. The snow had covered the vents completely and was melting through. There's four to four and a half feet of snow on our roofs, and that's compacted snow. One foot of it is ice.

The state sheriff flew in today and had coffee with us, but he did not say anything about the unlicensed cars sitting around.

Dad talked me into going sledding with him. The road grader was here and cleaned the roads, so it's good sledding. And it's downhill all the way to the dock. He bundled me up in his parka and gloves. We were gone about 15 minutes, and my face and hands were frozen.

No wind today, so it's beautiful. The sun was out early, but oh! how cold! It sure feels good to sit in the nice warm cabin. The lodge is cold.

January 14th:

It's a little warmer this morning, but the lodge is cold as ice. Guess what! Yes, the toilets and everything froze up. Our butter and syrup which was put on the table last night for use this morning didn't have much consistency. The butter wouldn't spread and the syrup wouldn't pour. So here they sat making jokes. The men had to get out and dig the snow off the buried oil tank so the park board could deliver oil.

Our kitchen ceiling started leaking again, and they are up there now chopping off the ice. I assure you there is never a dull moment!

The sheriff is back again. There is something wrong. I can feel it, and I hope it isn't what I think.

January 15th:

It warmed up last night and is snowing lightly. So the men are back to work. Dad's insulated underwear and snowmobile boots are keeping him nice and warm. Most of the men have problems keeping their feet warm.

Each night we sit around for a while and talk, especially right after dinner. Last night it was religion. When it comes to religion and politics, you had better watch out!

But this is really the only topic that you can learn and understand other people's feelings.

Before the conversation was over, everyone had really opened their hearts. Some, or rather 99%, said when they had problems, they went to church and prayed or prayed at home with their own families.

They said it didn't always solve every problem, but it at least released the tension. Then you did not worry as much and felt better.

Then Herb said, "Hell, when I worry about something, I just reach for a cigarette, and another cigarette, and another cigarette. So on through the day."

Then someone asked him if that relieved the tension.

"Hell, no!" he said. "Then my ulcer bothers me, and I am sick for days."

"Have you ever gone to church?" asked someone.

"Yes," he said, "but I feel so guilty sitting there, I won't go again. I guess it goes back to my childhood. I ran away from home at 17, got married, and joined the army."

The men did get a little work accomplished. Leslie Kearns went into Juneau to look over the town while it was so cold, but he got stranded for several days. He chartered out yesterday. I don't know how much it cost him, but it was plenty, as he was the only passenger. It was a good thing he did.

Last night we saw the movie "The Fierce Sea." It was good. And Thursday night we saw Walt Disney's "Dalmatians," and after the movies last night, we had a square dance at Gustavus. Fun was had by all!

January 16th:

Today is the most miserable, stormy, windy day of all. We have such a blizzard that we can hardly get back and forth to the lodge. The railed walkway is a godsend, or else you would be blown away. The wind is a-howling and whistling, and the buildings crack and groan. We have snow blown in our cabin door. It runs three feet from the door, and the snow is frozen.

I just now came from the lodge to the cabin because it is so cold in the lodge, and everyone is hovering around the fireplace. I might add it's the poorest fireplace for heat I have ever seen. It's beautiful but useless. Anyway, when I got to the cabin, the snow on my pants was frozen. We will probably get a report on the storm later on.

Now they are all listening to the game on our old radio which is the only one that works up here. I am going to nestle on the bed and finish *Airport*.

If you get away from the front door, the rest of our cabin is nice and warm, and at night for some reason it is terrible hot.

We only need a sheet for cover, even if it is 20 below at night. This is steam heat, and it builds up at night. If we survive this storm, we can survive anything. We took pictures but think it's too dark to take well.

Dinner time! The only warm place is the kitchen, but there is no room to eat in there. We have to eat in the dining room. I had to laugh even if I would have frozen to death. I would love to have had a moving camera. All of us women were dressed in our husbands' thermals. Then the problem was to find something big enough to wear over those bulky things. Well, I just did not have much except for my jeans, and every time I moved a muscle they would come unbuttoned. Over these we had a sweater and then a coat, plus our fleece-lined shoes. Here we all were, men included, sitting at the table at about 38° with our teeth a-chattering and trying to eat the once very hot food.

The wind just howled through those big windows. We ran Visqueen all through the lodge to cover all the windows. Otherwise, I believe we would have frozen. Our thermostat did not even register. The lowest number on it was 45°. I could hardly believe it, but our cabin was like ice, so two Kearnses and Dad and I went way up to the top lobby with all our clothes on. We weren't too uncomfortable, so we played cards until 10:30 pm.

January 17th:

What a night! We were cold for the first time at night, and it was zero. The park employees said with the chill factor it was about 40° below last night. They said it was the worst winter in over 40 years. There is twice as much snow as usual, and the wind has been terrific. So, no work again. Dad went out for a few minutes and came back with ice in his beard plus his ears about frozen off.

January 18th:

It is still miserable and cold and around zero degrees. But it's that horrible chill factor. The men's systems will not tolerate the weather. They can only tolerate the weather for a little while, and then they get real weak and have to come inside. They bundle up and do the necessary things such as fixing frozen pipes, toilets, and showers. This morning we had no hot water.

The cook and I have it real nice in the kitchen. Joe is a restaurant cook, and can only cook the few meals that are on the menu. As for a family group like we are here, he is absolutely lost and cannot compare to Andy.

All we get is chili pie, rolls, and fish. If my theory is right, he will not be here long.

The very polite officer is back, and he has Karl in a corner. I know he has dope here with him, as that is something you cannot hide forever. When Karl had his long hair hanging in his eyes, it wasn't so noticeable. Now that his hair is short and no longer in his eyes, his eyes have sort of a glassy, peculiar look. His roommate was also questioned.

What the goofy kid did was he did not want to be the only one on narcotics, so what does he do, but give it to two sisters, 15 and 17 years old, plus their 19-year-old brother. The parents of these kids detected it, turned in their own kids, and this is the reason for the interrogation. Karl has been on narcotics for some time and is very sly. So naturally, the kids all denied it, and there isn't anything they can do unless they find it on them. Karl has served time in California and is on parole.

What is the answer? Should there be more leniency, or should the punishment be more harsh so they think twice before doing it again. This is the discussion at the lodge and Gustavus where the family lives. There are seven children in this family, and the family wants Karl to leave so their children can grow up here in Gustavus where they have lived all their lives in peace and harmony. They are a very nice and close family and have always enjoyed the simple life.

January 19th:

Winter has settled in here in Glacier Bay. The wind has howled and whistled, and everything is frozen, even our washing machines. That's why I'm washing by hand.

January 21st:

Joe, our cook, goes into Juneau today to attend to some of his business, so I always automatically fall into head cook. He expects to be gone for five days.

It has cleared again, and we are now having normal Alaskan weather. The coldest so far has been 40 below with our chill factor. You have probably read about Juneau's storm and avalanche plus their 60 below. Some of the people are still without water. It sure paralyzes everything.

January 22nd:

As I stated before, Joe is a restaurant cook, and he fixes us chili every day. Before he left, he made us about four gallons of chili and gave me strict orders to have it for the men both at noon and at night. We are all so sick of chili, none of us can eat it. So I just set it in the refrigerator. He adds ground cumin to his chili and no tomato sauce. It is good, but you cannot eat it twice a day!

The crab men came in tonight and loaded us down with crab, as the crab season ends this month, and they are going south for a vacation. Then they'll come back to do commercial fishing in March.

We cleaned crab until 1:30 am and have the rest to clean today. They sure are fine men, and we here at the lodge sure appreciate the crab, as you know the price!

While we had this miserable weather up here last week, these fishermen were marooned on some island, and they about froze. So they left their motor and heater running. Anyway, somehow the boat got on fire on the starboard deck and nearly burned them up.

Now they are on their way to Wrangell to have the boat repaired while they are enjoying themselves for a while. These men claim it's a terrible hard life. They are always so grateful when it's over mainly because the weather on water in the winter time is terrible, especially here in Alaska.

January 23rd:

Everyone slept in this morning except for Dad. He went to work at 9:00 am, the rest came in for breakfast at 10:00 am, and went out to work at 11:00 am. It is a gorgeous, beautiful day, and since they only worked about two and a half days last week, they decided to work today, Sunday.

If only it wasn't so cold at times. Hands are the worst. We couldn't find any knitted gloves at home. They have to have fingers in them so you can handle nails. Frank is going to try to find some in Juneau. Dad had one pair, and they just lasted him one week. So it's a problem.

January 24th:

Are we ever enjoying the crab! We had crab cocktails and crab louie. Now we are going to try and deep fry some.

We had some Pinochle game! Dad and I played the Kearns brothers, and we played three hours on one game.

Since we only cleaned 1/3 of the crab, I tried to get the men to clean the rest of it, shuck it, and also boil it. But you never do today what you can do tomorrow. So, as usual, about $100 worth of crab spoiled. They are finally trying to save some of it. But we will not eat it, as crab has to be boiled while fresh. I am just now enjoying living, so I won't take a chance.

The weather is still beautiful, and the air is full of planes.

January 25th:

Today Joe, our cook, comes in, so I will just work four hours again. My letter writing takes a lot of time, as everyone wants to hear from us. So I really do not have any spare time at all. Some of the park employees come over and talk, and by the time you converse just a little with the 20 other people here plus playing cards etc. there just isn't such a thing as spare time.

January 26th:

We have had four days of beautiful weather and I mean beautiful! The men are making headway again. By the Juneau paper Centralia is underwater again by Riverside Park. You would think by now that would be old news. Everyone has had their share of bad weather.

January 27th:

The nice weather is still with us, and the men are going strong.

Our cook drinks a fifth of whiskey per day, and when he talks to you, he comes right up to you. When you yourself do not drink, that is pretty hard to take. I know the Kearnses do not know this. He is harmless, so let him drink up his money. I try not to converse with him too much.

January 28th:

I am afraid the weather will change, as it is cloudy today but warm. I brought some stationery that I will paint in my spare time.

We saw another movie tonight. Poitier in the "Valley of the Lily" or vice versa. We had the usual full house.

January 29th:

It has clouded up some, and we have about two inches of new snow. The trees look so exotic. John, our lather, slipped and hurt his back. Jim Kearns is still babying his knee, so the Bengay is going around quite strong. Some of the kids are going to the square dance tonight, and others are doing their personal washing. Some are playing cards. I am lazy and reading.

January 30th:

Sunday and everyone slept in. We had steak, fried potatoes, eggs, and toast for breakfast at 10:00 am, and then laid around all day. We had chicken dinner at 4:30.

The weather cleared up, and it's very nice again. Today was cabin cleaning for all plus changing bed linens. We do not have to wash our own bedding and towels, as that is done in the big laundromat by our washing lady.

Some of the boys went sledding, some went for walks, but most of us were very lazy.

Tonight as we were playing cards, the martens came to the door and watched us, but the minute we moved, they were gone. The squirrel sat on the steps eating away. By the way, his name is George. Last night he sat under our bedroom window chattering away.

I had all the luck in Pinochle tonight. We played two games, and I got every bid but two. Won one game in three hands. Needless to say, they were disgusted.

Yours Truly, The Carpenter's Wife

February 1st:

It warmed up today and it's snowing again. Nothing much happened, just the same old routine. It isn't too cold, and the project goes on.

We get to see one of those 30-year-old movies again tonight, but they are a riot, and we always have a full house. During the movie someone will holler out and say, "Hey! That one looks just like Chuck." Some of the men always have a remark to make if there is a well-shaped female. Once in a while it gets a little out of order.

There isn't much to write lately, so my notes will probably get shorter and shorter. We battle the snow day in and day out. Some have fallen and hurt themselves or got a few smashed fingers. Otherwise, everything is going okay, and I hope it will continue, as serious accidents we can do without.

These service people are an ambitious bunch of characters. After five months, they finally got the dishwasher fixed.

February 6th:

After two weeks of beautiful weather, we now have an Alaska blizzard again. Good thing it is Sunday, so let's hope it will blow over instead of lasting for nearly a week like it did the last time. I suppose if a person lived here and had to work for a living, the weather would really bother you. But with us, we can just sit and watch it, and it is really interesting to watch the snow. One minute it is blowing straight north. The next time you look, the snow is flying around in circles like a whirlwind. Then again it will blow west, or it can come down real straight. It isn't monotonous!

We shoveled and cleaned the sidewalks several times today, as drifts get three to four feet high, and we can't get back and forth from the cabin to the lodge which is about 200 feet. The snow is so dry and light that you sink down to the bottom, and it's very hard to walk in.

We got rid of our restaurant cook. Blah! It was hard to eat! So a consolation prize for a new cook. The new cook isn't really a new cook, just **yours truly, the carpenter's wife!** They offered me $800 a month plus room and board if I would cook lunch and dinner. I do not have to cook breakfast. And since I was doing it most of the time anyway, I thought I might just as well draw the pay, so I accepted. Not that I will be able to keep much of it. I am sure getting a lot of compliments on the food.

I really love Alaska and don't miss home at all!

February 8th:

If everyone keeps on eating like they have lately, they are going to kill themselves off. Gee, it takes a lot of food, and they want good food.

I made a big batch of bread today, and it turned out exceptionally good. I surprised myself!

It snowed one foot on Sunday, so we are up to five feet of snow again. The snow and ice is so heavy on the lodge that the roof is sagging, and it is splitting one side wall. Things are desperate, and they are doing something about it.

Dad got a telegram yesterday stating his (half) brother in St Louis passed away. Doctors don't know the cause. A good thing we went to see them last summer.

It warmed up after the blizzard and is raining. The native residents are afraid of what this will do. It will no doubt flood everything and wash the road out. You know, with all this bad weather, there has been only one day that there wasn't school. They know how to drive in the snow, therefore, no hindrance.

It was much nicer when everything was frozen instead of this mush.

February 10th:

It is still warm and raining. One of our deep freezes went haywire, and when everything was frozen, they did not worry about it. This morning I blew my top, and I told them I would not be responsible for several hundred pounds of food and meat going to waste just because they did not fix it. So I had to empty that big freezer and squeeze what I could into the other two, and they buried the rest in four feet of snow. How I wish you could have some of this luscious fish going to waste! That halibut and salmon just can't be beat.

Dan, our engineer, is coming this weekend, and he will make things fly around here. He knows what should be done, and he cracks the whip. There are a couple here that think he is too stern. But not me, I am all for him. He loves food, so I will have some help in the kitchen. He is a big 6'6" Norwegian or Swede. And he will also liven up the lodge.

February 11th:

These were two busy days. I baked a big, big batch of cookies and ten pies. I stuck a few into the deep freezer, as we never know when we will have company. Then I will have something to fall back on.

John Wayne was in our weekly movie Friday night. First, we usually make a big batch of popcorn, and this is passed around from aisle to aisle during the movie. It's hilarious, especially if the film breaks. These people here really have a good time, and they are also friendly and nice.

With the rain on top of the snow, the lodge roof started to sag more, and we thought for sure it was going to crash. We had to get up on it and shovel and shovel and shovel! It's a good thing it was built well.

Thank goodness, it's now back to cold again, as that is much better than the rain. The men are making good progress since they ordered heaters from Juneau.

February 12th:

Jack: It has been above freezing twice since the first of the year, and we still only have about four feet of snow. But it's been up around above 20° for several days, so it feels quite warm after being so cold before.

The planes are rather irregular here in the winter. They can only fly a day or two a week.

I am working inside of the cabins most of the time, so I'm quite comfortable. Mother is now the head cook and is kept awfully busy, but she seems to enjoy it. I haven't shaved or had a haircut for months. I was going to cut them off, but Mother thinks I look real handsome!

February 14th:

Leah: The marten finally performed for me. The snow by the kitchen window is higher than the window, so I was watching him from it, and he did not know it. They do not stay in one spot very long, and are they ever rapid! It would have made a beautiful moving film.

I get a kick out of Dad. He wants to shave so badly, yet he wants me to say so, so he can say I made him. But I am holding off and not saying a word. This really has him perplexed.

"You know, my long hair really bothers me," he keeps saying, hint, hint! He hasn't had a haircut since Christmas.

But I never say a word. His beard is quite long now, and he does have an unusual beard. It's just as curly as can be. They want him to keep his beard and stay around the lodge and be Sourdough Jack of Alaska! So I am keeping mum, and he can make his own decision.

There are no eaves or gutters here on the homes. So the frozen ice and snow hang over the edge of the buildings, and on our cabin it protrudes about three feet. Then the icicles go to the ground. It's very odd. We have one real big icicle that is about two square feet.

February 15th:

It warmed up today to above 30° and started to rain. The snow slid off the roof about one and a half feet, and finally our unique icicle went down. But the snow now protrudes about four and a half feet, and it covers over half of our window. I took some pictures, hope it wasn't too bright. Today I will take some in the snow storm so you can see our window before and after.

I sure wish I were an artist or at least knew a little about painting, as this is a paradise. If a person could paint all the mountains and the inlet of Glacier Bay, they would sell like hotcakes here at the lodge. A park serviceman's wife makes pottery out of the clay, and she cannot keep the lodge supplied.

February 16th:

I made a big batch of hamburger buns and weiner buns today. We had hot dogs for lunch. I put cheese on the inside and wrapped a piece of bacon around it. We had all the relishes, pickles etc. to put on them. Then the problem was how to eat them! A few men had big enough mouths! Anyway, they enjoyed them.

We always have guests here, and they never tell me. Today I blew my top. "If we have guests, after this I want to be told!" I said.

February 17th:

Surprise! I believe winter is just arriving! We woke up to one foot of new snow, and it is snowing hard plus a little wind. Three hours ago I made it to the lodge with no problems, as Ray had shoveled the sidewalks. Now it is 12:30, and I had a terrible time getting back to our cabin. It was knee to waist high again from the drifts.

Dad is doing finish work, so he doesn't have it too bad. But the plumbers have deep trenches dug to get under the cabins. When they brought in the lumber this fall, they thought a good place to store some would be underneath the cabins. Well, the snow is past our windows now. Therefore, they have to dig tunnels to get underneath the cabins where there is about five feet of storage space.

Need I explain how hard and complicated it is to get the lumber out and try to carry it in this small walkway that has to be cleared and widened every hour or so.

Most of the snow has drifted in and has fallen off the roofs, so that we are surrounded in about 12 feet of snow. It is so white that it has a bluish cast to it. The tree branches are just laden with snow, and it's downright beautiful. I am having a perfect ball!

February 18th:

Since I am head cook, I am treated royally. Besides, they had to lay off two boys. One flew home to Arizona, and Ray is staying here, as they will need him if the weather will ever clear. So he is helping me with the cleanup. That is, he cleaned all three ovens for me, the barbecue grill, the fan, and scrubbed the floor. So that just leaves me the actual cooking which is a cinch. I have it real easy until Ray helps the men again.

I haven't had a day off since January 3rd. In fact, I do not even know what day of the week it is. I was a week ahead of myself so had to go back one week, and if this winter keeps up, I am afraid we are going to be way behind. They may get the cabins done, but then there is the sewer that has to be done and also all those sidewalks, and you can't do it when there is eight to 12 feet of snow.

So if we have a break – that is, nice weather but no work – some of us will fly out and see more of Alaska. I have Dad working on a nice three-day vacation now. Since flying is the only way to travel in Alaska, you can cover a lot of territory in a short time.

Friday night: Just got back from the kitchen after my break from writing the above. They can have my helper back. He said he would clean the ovens, as he had done it before, so I felt confident and left him. Now on my return to check, he sprayed so much cleaner in the ovens that it ran down the front of the stoves and onto the floor. Need I write what happened? Yes, it ate off the finish on the front.

His remark was, "Oh, it doesn't hurt the stove any. It just doesn't look nice."

Then I checked behind him on the other things he was supposed to do. It's like a five-year-old's work! So I am going to tell them I will handle the kitchen by myself, as it will take me a half day to clean up the floor. Now I know why Dad does not want him out there with him. He is a lovely 22-year-old boy (pardon me, a man!), but he is as useless as you-know-what!

Have another movie tonight, but the storm is still continuing and will not have too many tonight. Ray did get the sidewalks shoveled, so they are clear.

It's 10:30 at night. We just got out of the movies. Dad and I were prepared to run to the cabin in this blizzard. We looked out of the door, and we both started to laugh. Then everyone wondered what we were laughing at and joined us. The blizzard had covered our walkway again, and it was filled with four feet of snow with no way to get to the cabin.

Herb said, "I'll go first. Jim and John follow. If we make it, the rest of you can follow."

The three started out, and we all just about died laughing. This is all just soft, fluffy snow, as it is just blown in. Have you ever tried to walk in four feet of soft snow? It's the oddest feeling. Anyway, they fell and we could see their arms fly trying to keep the snow off their faces. But they finally made it. So the rest of us made a train and followed. We had more fun. But, oh, how cold!

I told Jeanne, the breakfast cook, that she wouldn't have to worry about an early breakfast. But she gets up at 6:30 anyway and tries to get to the lodge. Naturally, the walkway was filled with snow by morning again. So she didn't exactly know where she was treading, being quite dark. At any rate, she said she walked, crawled, and rolled, as it is downhill. She made it, but she nearly froze.

When she was telling us about it this morning, she laughed and laughed, stating she will never forget that experience.

In order for the rest of us to make it, we dug a walkway from the end cabin to the roadway which is only about 50 feet instead of 200 feet of walkway. And the road grader was up early this morning and graded the road, so the kids could get to school. This was our method of getting to the lodge. The storm died down, the sun is out, and it's one of those beautiful days again.

The new snow broke off the big overhang on the cabins, so now we will start out afresh. There is at least six feet of snow on top of our roofs. I do not know how they stand up under it.

The park service man said this is the worst winter ever. I'm glad we are here in it. It's great!

February 19th:

It is a cold, clear, beautiful day. It stopped snowing, but the wind is blowing, and it's a-blowing the snow everywhere.

Noon break: I decided to take some pictures, as it is clear, and the snow is blowing all around. Hope the slides are good. First off, I couldn't get back to the lodge so decided to take the end cabin trail. When I got halfway back, I saw the park service had dug up their fuel pipe to put oil in it, and it's about 12 ft deep. I had to crawl into that and out the other side. I had just taken the camera, no gloves.

I took one picture of the back of our cabin and found out it was the last picture on that roll. I did not say anything out loud, but I assure you my thoughts were not very pleasant. I turned around and crawled down that slippery hole, fell down, got up, then fell again.

When I finally got out of there, I looked like a snowball. The reason I kept sliding and falling is I wear Dad's size 11 boots with my pant legs over them so they won't fill up with snow right away.

By the time I got back to the cabin my hands were frozen. Well, the problem was I still had to get back to the lodge and still wanted to take pictures, so I bundled up in everything I could lay my hands on and started out again. I stuck the camera in my pocket and buttoned up just so my eyes stuck out, and away I headed for that trail again.

I did not have any better luck the second attempt. But the point is I made it! I got to the road, took pictures of the men shoveling snow off of everything, and I said, "Gee, isn't this exotic." For some reason or other the men wanted to take me back and bury me in that hole. I told them some men sure were narrow-minded!

Later on, going to the lodge in Dad's big boots, I was very careful. Yet I slipped on the second step and fell flat on my back. I heard something crack. It was either my back or the steps! Ray had just cleaned up the walkway. There was no soft snow for padding, and I hit terrible hard. But I slept fairly well through the night.

Today is Saturday. I cooked and made it through to lunch. Then my hip hurt me so bad I had to go to bed which is where I am now.

It was nice this morning, but I am afraid there is another blizzard starting up.

February 23rd:

A lot of water has run over the dam since I wrote last. I hurt my back in my fall, so they flew me to Juneau where a car waited for me and Dad. They took me to the emergency room at the hospital, x-rayed me, and found no broken bones. But I have one vertebrae that's slipped against the other, and I have a pinched nerve.

I fell on Friday but could not get to Juneau until Monday, Washington's birthday, and everything was closed. But the Kearns' doctor came to the hospital to see me. Since this is out of the doctor's line, naturally I wasn't helped much. He just gave me some pain pills and some exercises to do, and they do help.

Dad's boss gave him the day off with pay so he could go with me plus paid his plane fare. It was a beautiful day, and Dad rode up front with the bush pilot in a beautiful new six-passenger Piper.

On the return it was real rough, and we had to strap ourselves in real tight. When you hit those air pockets, you fly up to the ceiling and back down in such a hurry. To me it was a great thrill!

But to Sally Kearns it is very annoying, as she hates flying. Her baby isn't due until March. But since the weather has been so unpredictable, we all agreed she must fly to Juneau, rough or not, as none of us wanted to be a midwife.

So two days before I fell, we talked her into going to Juneau, and lo and behold! It was one of those rough flying days, and the baby was born the following day three weeks prematurely. It weighed seven pounds, but it could not breathe on its own. It had to have oxygen, but after one week, they think it will make it. They do not know what it had or the cause.

The whole family wanted a boy so there would be four boys and four girls. Well, it was a girl. Such disappointment at first. Now they don't care, just so she will live.

What a close family! I have never seen anything like it. The 20-year-old daughter in Utah is coming here to see the baby. The 18-year-old son is supposed to be in Arizona, but he won't leave here until his mother is at home, and the baby is okay.

I assure you Queen Elizabeth was never treated as royally as Sally.

The weather is something else again but very interesting. I was talking to the park service superintendent, and he said this was the worst winter on record. So far we have had 250 inches of snow (over 20 feet), and now we have 74 inches on the ground. The latest report is we will go home in mid April and come back after the snow is all gone to finish the job. So we have ordered our new pickup just in case.

I think that break will be kind of nice. We can take our time when touring Alaska later on.

February 26th:

I have been quite busy so have missed a few days. They found out what was wrong with Sally's baby. They found Sally had just turned diabetic, and the baby had complications. If it had been a full term baby, it would not have lived. Therefore, everyone is grateful for forcing her to fly on a turbulent day since it saved her baby's life. Everyone hates to fly on rough days, but I just love it.

We have had three miserable cold days again, and last night no one could spread their butter or pour their honey. They eat honey by the gallons here on their hot bread. We ate with all our coats on and our teeth a-chattering. Yet we had to have cobbler a la mode!

Herb, the contracting boss, is quite a guy! Yesterday he came into the kitchen and said, "By God, today I deserve my coffee! Is there any?"

I looked at him, and his eyebrows were singed, and his face all red. I said, "What happened to you?"

One of the new propane heaters had exploded and set the cabin on fire. The handy fire extinguisher saved the cabins. Luckily, Herb was standing or rather working at the right place where it hadn't hurt him, but it sure scared the daylights out of him.

He yelled, "Fire!" and everyone jumped. He thought everything was going to burn up.

The big shots were here looking at the damage and also checking into my injury. Since I am working for the lodge, I am supposed to be insured. I believe I will fly to Juneau to see if I can get a chiropractic treatment. It is very seldom that they can help me.

I walk around in pain, although the pain pills do help. But I am about out of them. Decisions, decisions, and more decisions!

Our weather cleared today and it is beautiful, not a breeze.

February 27th:

Sunday: A lazy, relaxing day for the men and everyone but me. I never get a day off. Now that mom and baby are okay, son Jeff Kearns left for Arizona. But her daughter Joan is still here from Utah.

The local talent put on a drama last night here at the lodge. Most of the Kearns kids were in it. It lasted two hours. They were all very good. Their one teacher is really clever and talented.

Frozen!

March 4th:

It has been one day less than a week since I have added to my notes. Everything has been running smoothly, even the weather has been accommodating, so all is well.

Friday night being movie night, last night we saw one of John Wayne's movies again. John Wayne is quite a fan of the Kearnses, as this is one of his fishing and drinking spots. They say he is the same in real life as in the movies.

Dad and I were sitting in front of the Masons. After the first half of the movie, Bill pipes up and says, "Gee, here I thought the picture was out of focus, and all I was doing was looking through Allender's beard. No wonder everything looked curly and fuzzy." He's such a character!

The weather has changed today. It is still warm, but it has started to snow. All of a sudden without any warning we lost our water at the lodge. The park service men are here on their snowshoes trying to find out what happened. You do not dare walk off the trails. It seems so funny to see them work on these snowshoes, but it's their only safe bet. During this warm week we have lost about one foot of snow, I think. I do not believe it is quite as high by our window. It didn't melt, it's just more compact.

The six inch water line finally froze up, so more problems. But this is a park service problem. Thank goodness we have water in our cabins yet.

March 7th:

The weather has cleared, and it is cold, cold again with our chill factor. It is or was 30 below last night. Our water main is still frozen and very likely will be until it thaws in the spring. The park department men were going to solve the problem and use the fire hose for our water hose. They laid it right on top of the snow. It wasn't but a couple of hours, and it was so frozen to the snow that the only way they would ever remove it would be to chop it out.

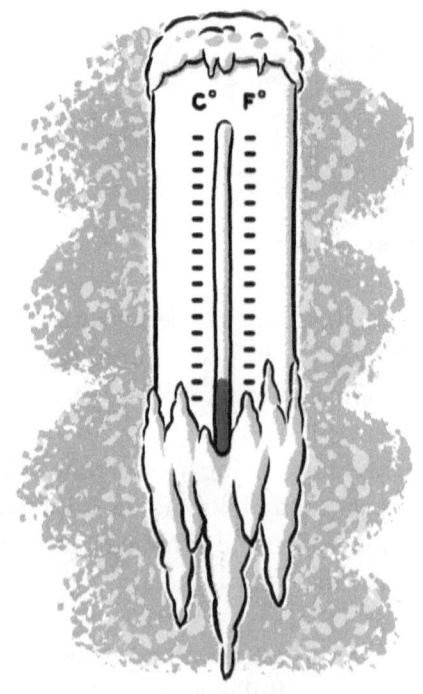

Then the Kearns brothers took hoses and wrapped it in insulation and buried it into the snow.

That so far has frozen up once a day, so that is dug up, and the hose put into the basement to thaw during the night and replaced during the day. That is two men's half day's work each day in this cold. Now I believe Dad has them finally convinced that they will have to leave one faucet run full capacity in order for it not to freeze. The test is on today!

With this cold they cannot tape or plaster, so we may have to go home sooner for our break than we thought.

We had a little more snow, it is as clear as a bell, the sun is bright, and the mountains are blue white. Beautiful! Dad and I both love it. Herb, the boss, hates it with a passion, as he is so homesick for his wife and child.

I slipped on the kitchen floor and caught myself, and I believe the vertebrae I got out when I fell on the snow slipped back in or so it feels. I hope! Now I am just terribly sore.

Mail day today so everyone was patiently waiting for the mail plane. We heard from my sister, the brother who just got married, several nieces and nephews, and a brother-in-law.

March 8th:

We have fought weather, tempers, heat, and now no water at all! You can't say we did not fight to the end! The end is here, and we are flying home tomorrow, as we can't live without water. Goodbye to Alaska until the weather changes for the better.

March 10th:

We are still in unpredictable Alaska. We were supposed to have left Thursday morning, but Wednesday night the big storm came, is still upon us, and is predicted through the weekend. So we are really snowbound, the worst of all. We are living out of one suitcase, as the others are packed and sitting at the lodge. It has really been comical. All the men are packed, dressed, and waiting for the seaplane, as they could come on a half hour's notice.

Since Dad and I both love it here, we do not care whether we go home or not. We both have been working as usual. Dad says there's lots of carpenter work to be done. So he will work and let some of the rest get the ulcers by sitting around.

We went to Sally Kearns' baby shower today at a park service man's home about a half mile from the lodge. Myke Mason and I walked there in the storm after two truck attempts in getting us there both got stuck. The wind has calmed down, so it was nice walking in a foot of new snow.

We now have running water at intervals. I never knew water could be so precious. Dad is over having his coffee and a sundae. I decided to skip mine tonight.

I hear his return footsteps. He was talking to the park service men, and they said no jets out of Juneau today. One is stranded at Sitka, another at Ketchikan, and they all have to wait until the storm is over before they can take off. You know these little planes and bush pilots do not have a chance in this weather.

We gave up on our walkway, so it's quite a chore to get to the lodge.

March 11th:

I just got the bread set and was notified the Grumman Goose* will be here in a few minutes to take us to the airport, so maybe we will get out of here yet.

We fishtailed to Juneau. The Juneau airport is a regular skating rink. We were on the standby list and got out on the second plane. We had a rough landing at Sitka, a good landing at Ketchikan. The weather is clearing, so we should have a smooth landing in Seattle. We will be back to civilization for several weeks. There was seven feet of snow at the lodge today.

* See #7 in 'A Little Extra' for more about bush floatplanes.

Help!

May 1st:

We have been back in Alaska for two busy weeks. The weather this week has been gorgeous, and the snow is melting fast, only one foot now on the ground. But we have many piles up to eight feet yet.

Tourist season will open on May 15th, we have 200 people coming that day, and the tourist season cook does not arrive until June 5th. And I might add I am petrified at the thought! They are afraid I might quit, so are treating me quite royally. There will be 25 workers here next week and 30 the following week. They are giving me help in the kitchen. Mollie and our friend Marian are flying up to help me for a while.

We are supposed to be done by the 26th of May, that is, the carpenters. They think they will make it, but we do not believe the sewer people will get done in time. We are kidding the Kearnses and telling them they will have to notify their guests and have them bring their own private portable stool, or else build an outhouse.

I had new help in the kitchen yesterday, and everything she did went wrong. When washing dishes, she broke several glasses. When she went to make coffee in the big coffee pot, she spilled what was left over on herself and me. When she was washing windows, she moved the ladder with the bucket sitting on top, and now she has a big lump and cut on her forehead. Poor girl! I felt so sorry for her. I told her just to slow down and not worry, as we all have days like that. I believe she will be real good help.

We will be here through June 1st for sure and haven't decided what we will do then. Dad can work in Juneau for the same company, but wants no foreman job, as he would rather not have the worries. Time will tell.

The bears have come out of hibernation so have them to contend with.

On our return to Juneau we stayed and toured the town, went to the Red Dog Saloon, and then to a restaurant for lunch. After looking at the menu, we decided all we could afford was a hamburger which was $1.75.

The town of Juneau is built on a hillside of solid rock, and the crummiest place rents for $150 to $425 per month. A two-bedroom duplex costs $350 per month. There is a terrible shortage of housing. Everything is half again as high as elsewhere. I was going to do some shopping but not at those prices!

It is 9:30 pm and the sun is still quite high. It should set at about 10:00 pm tonight, and it doesn't get dusk until about 11:00 pm. Therefore, you can't sleep! I hope to get used to it. The days are long, and the men are working 12 hours per day. I just came to the cabin after boiling my material for making ice cream. We now have our own ice cream freezer, the old-fashioned hand type, and I want chocolate ice cream for dessert tomorrow night. Do they ever go for that!

May 5th:

I just got through feeding 24 for lunch. Then Sally comes up and says, "I am sorry, Leah. They called from Juneau, and there are five Japanese guests coming for a 2:30 lunch."

My heart sank clear to the tip of my toes. All my lunch was being devoured in 24 stomachs. There is never anything left!

I said, "What can I fix in a half hour?" Then I thought, "Well, you are going to get a good old American sandwich! Like it or not!"

I got them bacon, lettuce, and tomato sandwiches with a fancy dish of pickles, celery, carrots, and fresh apples surrounding the compote of stuffed olives. I had fresh cupcakes left from our lunch and apricots. They thought it quite the lunch! They thanked me very kindly for that! They were all in their middle twenties.

We have a small group of guests coming in Friday again. There should be about 35 of us. Man, does it ever take the food! Will I be glad when Mollie arrives tomorrow to help me. I cooked for 28 today all by myself, plus baked ten loaves of bread, and I am exhausted tonight. They ate three and a half loaves of fresh bread alone plus each a big steak and all the trimmings. The nine cents a pound air freight on my last week grocery bill alone was $150 just to have it flown from Juneau to here. Our moose is all gone, so we have to buy all our meat, and that is heavy! The weight adds up!

I have just about read all of Alistair MacLean's books, believe I have one left. I like the way he writes. I read through all my breaks and until 11:00 pm every night. But Dad still reads three books to my one. He makes me so mad! Big excitement outside so must investigate....

May 10th:

Back again, but cannot remember what the big excitement was about when I closed above.

Mollie and Marian arrived, so now I can take life a little easier. The weather has been very accommodating, and it has been absolutely beautiful the last ten days. Mollie is really enjoying it here.

We went on the boat excursion, my second day off, and everything was perfect. The skipper, food, weather, and even the wild animals accommodated us. We got to within 20 feet to a mama goat* and her kid. The skipper shut off the motor, we coasted into the shore, and mama goat and her kid just stood there and watched us. Their fur was long and beautiful and white. Mollie thinks Alaska is more beautiful than Europe and I believe so, too.

The men will start fishing as soon as they get the boats in the water. They just got them dug out from under the snow. It is midnight and my bedtime, so will close.

See #8 in 'A Little Extra' for more about the mountain goat.

May 12th:

We had a real pretty sunset tonight at 10:00 pm. It seems so funny to have just four hours of dusk, as it really doesn't get dark. A person really gets in a lot of working hours! The men still work 11 to 12 hours per day, seven days a week. But they have a 10:00 am break plus a 3:00 pm. Then they go back to work after dinner, as the evenings are so long. They come to the lodge at 9:00 pm, and we all watch the sunset at 10:00 pm plus have another snack.

I am cooking for 32 people, and thank goodness Mollie and Marian arrived to help me. Work is a little easier. The weather has been perfect for the last ten days, and the snow has really melted. We have only about two feet up to eight feet piles left.

We hope to be through in June and can stay all summer but decided we should maybe go home. The Kearnses want Dad and me both up here next winter to remodel the lodge, and he also wants to go moose hunting up here.

May 19th:

Time flies and I never seem to get to my daily notes lately. We are cooking for 45 working men plus the guests, so I am putting in 12 hours every day seven days a week. I notified them that it was too many hours, that I could no longer do it, and that I needed a day off. Plus only eight hours a day. So, this is agreed.

It is 11:15 pm and is dusk, but it never gets dark during the summer. Mollie and Marian will head home after spending two weeks with me. Mollie enjoyed herself very much but wouldn't want my job for all the gold in China!

We still have quite a bit of snow, so the sewer men will be here longer than expected and so will we. We will take it as it comes.

I got three Mother's Day cards on the same day last week. I felt very proud of all three of my children that day. Even Dad strutted around like a peacock!

The men are still working 12 hours per day seven days a week, and it's beginning to tell on them. Hope they can last a couple of more weeks. The weather has been beautiful and accommodating.

Mail tomorrow so must get this off.

May 20th:

Dad and Marian went fishing the other night. They caught two dollies, one about 20 inches long. They are just coming into the bay, so fishing should be good in another week.

Mollie and Marian flew home after spending two hard-working weeks with me. The most we had to cook for were 72 people a day. Frank Kearns* was very pleased with Mollie and Marian's work. He paid for their airplane trip at $150 each, their bush pilot flights both ways for $60, their pleasure trip over the glaciers for $25, and their $25 boat excursion. Both were just thrilled to death to have such a nice vacation and all paid for! Even the weather accommodated.

They replaced Mollie and Marian with their three boys plus a kitchen supervisor. So now I am the baker, do nothing but the baking, and also cut down to eight hours per day. It's like I explained to them, "When you get my age, 12 hours a day and seven days a week is just too much."

* See '#9 A Little Extra' for information on Frank Kearns and Glacier Bay Park history.

Our working crew alone is 45 men, as they want to get done the 26th. But they won't make it. Dad will get finished with his, but the rest won't. Yet we will be the last ones to leave, as there will be lots of touch-up work after everyone leaves.

One of our guests caught a 70 lb halibut today. Is that ever a big fish! Was he thrilled, especially being from Nebraska.

As usual, I did my writing while resting or rather lying in bed. Hope you can make out parts of this anyway.

Sunsets

June 14th:

Thirty-six years ago today at 4:00 pm, we said, "I do. For better or worse!"

Our snow is melting fast, have about two feet left. Our squirrel is getting fat, our martens have left us, and I haven't seen the bear as yet.

Do we ever have beautiful sunsets! Everyone is busily taking pictures. It is after 10:00 pm and still very bright. I am sleepy and tired, but it seems so odd to go to bed in daylight.

We have been here nine months, and I have loved it all. But now I am ready to go home.

A Little Extra

#1 - Leah's Pumpkin Bread Recipe

Want to try Leah's pumpkin bread which was such a hit with the crew? It's doubtful she had a formal recipe, but here's one that will suffice. Her batch would have been larger and may have included a gallon can of pumpkin pie filling. Try substituting cranberries for raisins, pecans for walnuts. Or add mini chocolate chips.

Ingredients:

2 cups flour
1 teaspoon baking soda
½ teaspoon baking powder
½ teaspoon salt
1 ½ teaspoon ground cinnamon
1 teaspoon ground nutmeg
½ teaspoon ground cloves
¾ cup unsalted butter, softened (1 ½ sticks)
2 cups sugar
1 15 ounce can pumpkin puree (not pumpkin pie filling)
2 large eggs
1 cup golden raisins
½ cup walnuts, chopped

Instructions:

Preheat the oven to 350 degrees. Grease two loaf pans with cooking spray, set aside.

In a medium bowl combine dry ingredients, through cloves. Mix with a whisk to combine.

In a large bowl cream the butter and sugar with a mixer. Add in the pumpkin and eggs and mix to combine. Fold in the dry ingredients to combine then stir in the raisins and walnuts.

Pour the mixture into the prepared pans using a rubber spatula to smooth the tops. Bake for 55-60 minutes, until a toothpick inserted in the center comes out clean. Cool on a wire rack for at least 10 minutes before cutting.

#2 - Leah's Tin Can Christmas Tree

Although not mentioned in her letters, this craft project was a Leah favorite back home along with her egg carton Christmas tree. This project uses cans with end seams on top and bottom.

1.) Start with 11 seven ounce empty tuna (or similar) cans. Remove the bottom lid, strip labels, and clean thoroughly. (Many modern cans, unlike in 1971, only have a top seam for using a can opener. Without a seam on the bottom, removing it may not be practical, so just leave it on.)

2.) Place a straight wood cleat on a workbench, and line up four cans on their backs against the cleat.

3.) Solder the cans where they touch by using a rosin core solder and an electric solder gun.

4.)   Flip over the cans and repeat the solder on the other side. (If using cans without the bottom seam, skip this step.)

5.)   Now center three more cans above the initial four and settle them into the notches of the four cans.

6.)   Next, solder them to each other and to the four initial cans and on both sides.

7.)   Repeat this process with two more cans and then one last can.

8.)   One more step is to stand up the tree and set it on top of the 11th can which is lying flat on the bench.

9.)   Center well and solder to the tree at four locations.

10.)   If all has gone well, the tree should stand up and be ready for decorating!

11.)   Decorating can consist of spray painting the tin cans, or not.

12.)   Purchase smaller round Christmas tree balls of a size that fit into the can opening with their tree hook loop intact.

13.)   Slip a bobby pin over the top of the can and through the ball hook loop.

14.)   Repeat for all ten cans.

15.)   Voila, you have Leah's Christmas tree! (Jack was enlisted to do the soldering!)

#3 - Black Bear

From her cabin window, Leah watched a black bear mama teach her cub crucial tree-climbing skills. Next to mama, a tall tree is a black bear cub's best friend. Typically, that tree will be a white pine with a thick trunk and many strong branches, enough to hold cubs and mama when threatened.

After scratching out a nest at tree base for her growing cubs, the female will roam the area, leaving them to play there, near enough to climb high to safety if need be.

Today, black bears frequent the Bartlett Cove area. Always black, these bears? No, fur colors vary from black to brown to tan. Instead, look for these features to distinguish a black bear: a flat back with no shoulder hump, a prominent nose and ears. And big, up to 300 pounds of big!

#4 - Bush Pilots

The term "bush" originated as a British term for vast undeveloped lands in Africa. Because Alaska does, indeed, have a vast "bush" country, there are lots of bush pilots in Alaska, over one percent of the population or some 9000.

Career pilots transporting the general public for a fee must hold a commercial license. This requires from 500 to 1500 training hours, depending upon the type of license, to receive a Federal Aviation Administration certificate. An instrumentation rating allows flying in more difficult conditions. Private pilots require only 80 training hours but can not provide commercial services.

Bush pilots fly in unpredictable, often dangerous weather conditions over difficult terrain to transport locals, workmen, tourists, sportsmen, and supplies. All can tell tales of elation and terror. Although Alaskan pilots have a higher death rate than those in the lower 48, this rate has dropped significantly over the years.

#5 - American Marten

So fascinating to Leah, the marten is part of the weasel clan. Adults, distinguished by their black eyes and roundish faces and ears, measure up to a couple feet long including a long tail. Marten bibs are lighter colored, often yellowish, with a darker brown to black body and feet.

Excellent swimmers and tree climbers, these critters weigh up to four pounds. Their slim bodies and large furry feet let the marten lope easily through heavy snow without sinking.

Except in the June-to-August mating season, martens are solitary mammals. But around other martens, they communicate with body posture and chuckles, huffs, and shouts.

It's pretty doubtful that Leah fed mice or red squirrels to her martens, but those are dining favorites along with voles and other small creatures, berries, and nuts.

#6 - Red King Crab

The Alaskan red (dark red to burgundy) king crab is one of the largest crabs. Males can weigh up to 25 pounds and span five feet. Leah would not have had a pot large enough to boil this one!

The females can carry thousands of embryos under a tail flap for a year before they hatch as swimming larvae. The larvae feed on plankton for several months before drifting to the ocean floor, finally forming baby crabs of about one-half inch across.

King crabs are omnivorous scavengers that feed on mollusks, fish, and algae. With a lifespan of up to 30 years, these crabs must shed (molt) their hard shells multiple times as they grow.

Crabs are a high demand gourmet seafood. Thus, they are highly fished with open fishing season from October to January. Fishermen work long hard hours to maximize their harvest, often encountering stormy weather and dangerous conditions.

Just watch an episode of "Deadliest Catch" as they battle freezing temperatures, 40 foot waves, high winds, and 700 pound crab pots out in the Bering Sea! Maybe Leah would have found that fun, also!

#7 - Bush Floatplanes

Floatplanes transport large numbers of guests, workers, supplies and mail to and from Glacier Bay Lodge. Many of the same models of planes that flew Leah and Jack are still the mainstay today. A few of the floatplanes that frequent the lodge are listed below.

DeHavilland Beaver: In production from 1947 to 1967, the Beaver has a range of 450 miles at up to 140 mph. It can carry six passengers or 2,000 pounds of cargo. These are still flying by the hundreds. The plane has the oil reservoir filler located in the cockpit, so during cold weather the oil could be filled during flight. Built in Canada with a service life of over 70 years, the Beaver was considered to be the best bush plane to fly Alaska,

DeHavilland Otter: The Otter, the newer and larger brother of the Beaver, was built between 1952 and 1967. It's capable of a 900 mile range at 155 mph with up to 11 passengers or 3500 pounds. Of the 466 built, 165 are still flying. An Otter crossed the South Pole in 1957 as part of the Trans-Atlantic Expedition.

Grumman Goose: Known as a flying boat, the Goose was produced from 1937 to 1945, and, of the original 345, a couple dozen still fly today! They can range up to 650 miles at a cruising speed of 190 mph while carrying six passengers or 2500 pounds of cargo. The Goose was truly an odd duckling with its fuselage designed to act as the pontoons during water landings.

#8 - Mountain Goat

An impressive sight Alaska visitors hope to see? Mountain goats. Even better, a mama and her kid navigating the rocky terrain above the waters of Glacier Bay.

These hoofed animals stand up to three feet tall and can weigh upwards of 200 pounds. Visible, the mountain goat's thick white fur and black spiky horns. Not visible, the design of their amazing hoof.

Two large, independent hoofed toes have hard outer shells. Inside, a stretchy pad-like suction material can grip any surface. Those toes help them evade predators – wolves, bears, wolverines. Advantage, mountain goat!

Nannies, the term for female goats, typically give birth to one kid. And that baby is soon comfortable roaming the rocks with mama.

What a thrill for Leah and her sister Mollie, seeing two goats up close as their tour boat drifted through Glacier Bay waters.

#9 - Online Reference Material:

Land Reborn: A History of Administration and Visitor Use in Glacier Bay National Park and Preserve by Theodore Catton.

Want more? This soup-to-nuts history of the Glacier Bay area covers it all. The early Tlingit residents, the importance of nearby Gustavus' airfield in WWII, the 1925 establishment of Glacier Bay National Monument.

View online by searching for the title. The history of Frank Kearns' involvement in the lodge is included in Chapter VIII, The Glacier Bay Concession.

Finally, in 1980, the monument became Glacier Bay National Park and Preserve. Maps, historical pictures, tables, acronyms – all sorts of fascinating information about this unique region.

Leah Allender – Circa 1956

Biography

Leah Schneider Allender was born in Kansas in 1916 to German immigrant farmers and moved with her family to Garard Creek near Oakville, WA, when she was ten. The middle child of eleven, she helped support the family by caring for younger children, cooking, and picking ferns to sell for funeral home use. The post-Depression period necessitated her withdrawal from school after the eighth grade but left her with a strong work ethic and solid survival skills.

Neighbor Jack Allender, whose father was more established and prosperous, had access to his father's new car for courting Leah, and they married in 1936 when both were about 20. Children — Betty, Ed, and Ken — and, eventually, seven grandchildren, and several great-grandchildren completed the Allender family.

In 1945 the family moved to Fords Prairie north of Centralia where Jack built a home and established a 12-acre farm with barns, beef cattle, a milking cow, chickens, rabbits, a pig, some sheep, and the occasional horse. Butchering, canning, preserving, plus introducing the Sunday dinner chicken to the chopping block — all part of Leah's life as a farm wife.

Leah remained close to her siblings and their growing families. Over the years her clan gathered for special occasions, requiring her and her sisters to organize and feed the throng.

Leah managed home and children, attended school sporting events, tended to vegetable and flower gardens, and won garden club awards for her floral arrangements. And she enjoyed weaving rugs, quilting bedspreads, and making Christmas decorations from throw-away materials such as pine cones, dried weeds, and empty tuna cans.

Following this Alaskan adventure, Jack and Leah drove their camper to all 50 states, spent relaxing winters in Yuma, AZ, and summered in Centralia where Jack built a smaller home and grew dahlias.

Jack died in 1999 and Leah in 2000. They are buried in Centralia, WA.

SENTON DESIGN

@SENTONDESIGN / SENTONDESIGN.COM

www.sentondesign.com/books/lftcw

sentondesign@gmail.com